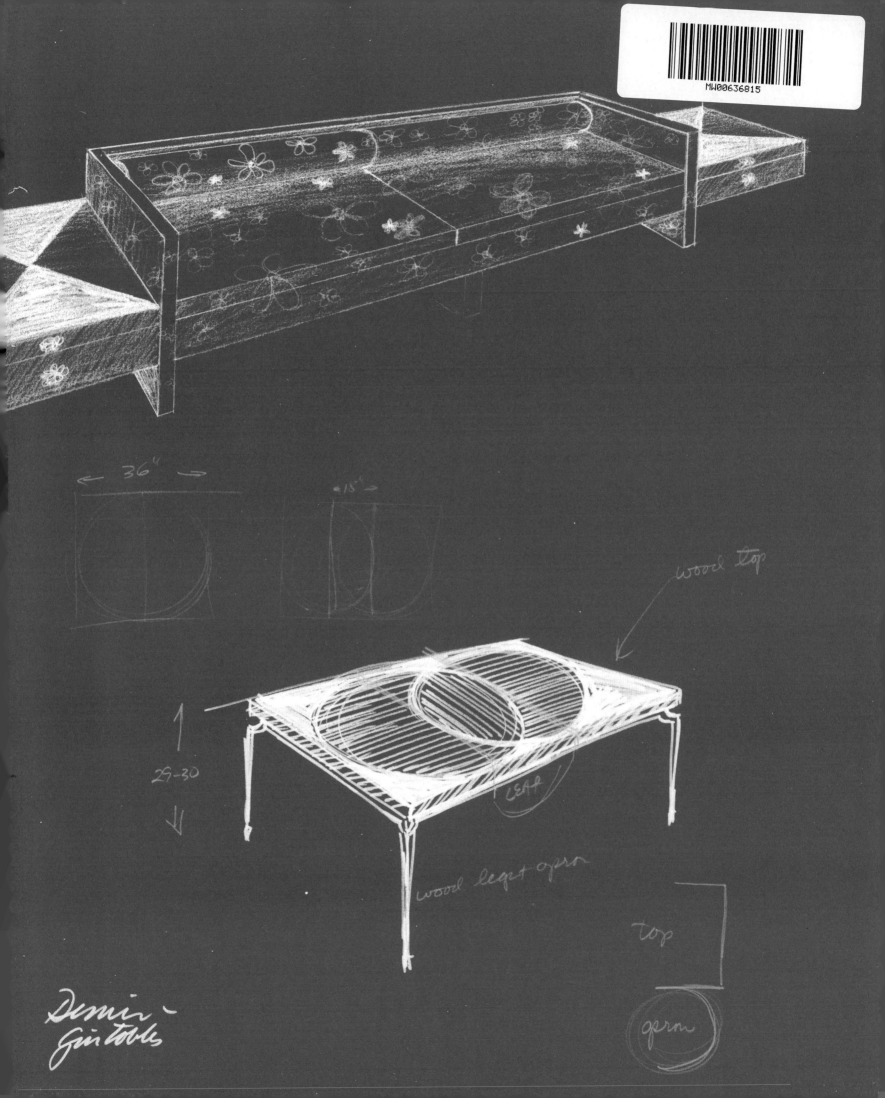

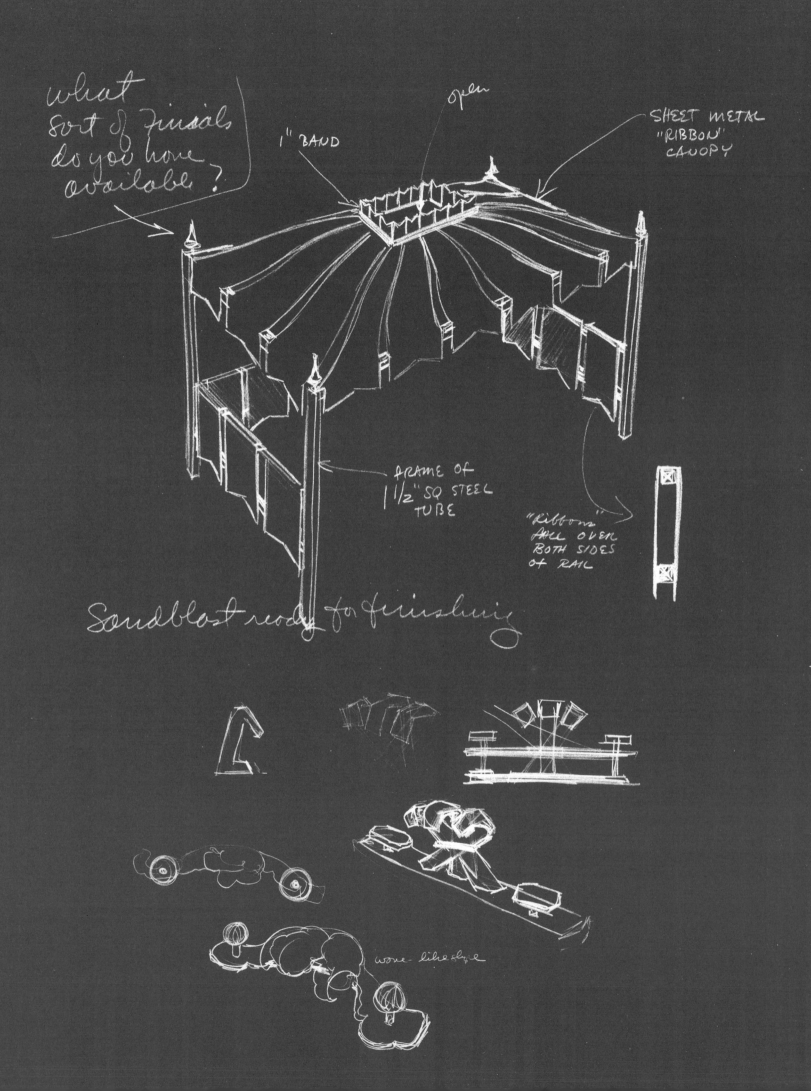

what
sort of finials
do you have
available?

open

1" BAND

SHEET METAL
"RIBBON"
CANOPY

FRAME OF
1 1/2" SQ STEEL
TUBE

"Ribbons"
fall over
both sides
of rail

Sandblast ready for finishing

wave-like style

ARTHUR ELROD
desert modern design

To Scott —
Viva Palm Springs
~ all things Elrod!
Adèle

ARTHUR ELROD
desert modern design

adele cygelman

GIBBS SMITH
TO ENRICH AND INSPIRE HUMANKIND

PREVIOUS PAGE: Arthur Elrod's Lanai/Beach Cabana with all-weather upholstery, vinyl floors, and outdoor grill was originally installed at the 1st Annual Palm Springs Decorators & Antique Show and Sale, which launched in 1961 at the Palm Springs Playhouse, and then reinstalled in 1962 at a New York design show. BELOW: A guest bedroom in publisher Duane and Marsha Hagadone's summer lake house shows Elrod's mastery of bold colors and multiple patterns.

First Edition
23 22 21 20 19   5 4 3 2 1

Text © 2019 Adele Cygelman
For photography credits, see page 220

Published by
Gibbs Smith
P.O. Box 667
Layton, Utah 84041

1.800.835.4993 orders
www.gibbs-smith.com

Designed by Kurt Wahlner
Printed and bound in China

Gibbs Smith books are printed on either recycled, 100% post-consumer waste, FSC-certified papers or on paper produced from sustainable PEFC-certified forest/controlled wood source. Learn more at www.pefc.org.

Library of Congress Cataloging-in-Publication Data

Names: Cygelman, Adele, author.
Title: Arthur Elrod : desert modern design / Adele Cygelman.
Description: First edition. | Layton, Utah : Gibbs Smith, [2019] | Includes
   bibliographical references and index.
Identifiers: LCCN 2018032233 | ISBN 9781423648789 (hardcover : alk. paper)
Subjects: LCSH: Elrod, Arthur, 1924-1974. | Interior
   decorators–California–Biography. | Interior
   decoration–California–History–20th century. | Modern movement
   (Architecture)–California–History–20th century.
Classification: LCC NK2004.3.E55 C94 2019 | DDC 747.092 [B] –dc23
LC record available at https://lccn.loc.gov/2018032233>
ISBN 13: 978-1-4236-4878-9

CONTENTS

INTRODUCTION

No one outside Palm Springs knows Arthur Elrod's name. But everyone knows the Elrod House, created for him by architect John Lautner and completed in 1968. And if you don't know the Elrod House by name from having seen photos of it published endlessly in magazines or online, then you surely know it from a memorable sequence in the 1971 James Bond movie, *Diamonds Are Forever*.

Arthur Elrod was the most successful interior designer working in the Palm Springs area from 1954 to 1974. His firm, Arthur Elrod Associates, completed countless projects in the desert and across the United States. He designed vacation homes, main homes, second homes, third homes, model homes, spec houses, and designer showhouses.

His rise paralleled the growing modernist movement in desert architecture, and he worked alongside the leading California architects of the day—E. Stewart Williams, William F. Cody, Paul R. Williams, Buff & Hensman, A.

Quincy Jones, Wexler & Harrison, Palmer & Krisel, Howard Lapham, Richard Dorman, Edward Fickett and, most famously, John Lautner.

He respected architects, and they respected him. His clients adored him. And yet, apart from the Elrod House, very little is remembered about his design practice. Unlike architecture, which stands a reasonable chance of surviving intact or being restorable, interiors are rarely found unchanged 50 years on. And interior designers are often given short shrift in academic circles, not taken as seriously as architects and rarely accorded the acclaim they deserve. Elrod is a prime example of an interior designer whose work was ahead of its time and published extensively, and yet he has become a footnote in design history.

His life was cut short by a tragic accident. But over those 20 golden years of Arthur Elrod Associates, magic was created. It's time to bring Arthur Elrod and his work out of the shadows and return him to his rightful place as one of the most influential designers of the twentieth century.

Arthur Elrod photographed at the home of Ann Peppers in Redlands ca. 1959 when he was in his mid-30s. His immaculate appearance—suits always impeccably tailored, never a hair out of place—was as important to him as the personal attention and innovative environments that he provided for his clients.

It takes a small army to bring archival material to life. My heartfelt thanks to everyone who contributed to this book.

For archival research and photography:
• The archive of Arthur Elrod Associates, Inc., and Harold C. Broderick is housed in the Lorraine Boccardo Archive Study Center at the Palm Springs Art Museum, Architecture and Design Center. This book would not exist without the support and assistance of Brooke Hodge, Director of Architecture and Design, and Frank D. Lopez, Archivist/Librarian. www.psmuseum.org/architecture-design-center/
• Jeri Vogelsang and Renee Brown, Palm Springs Historical Society, Welwood Murray Memorial Library. www.palm-springshs.pastperfectonline.com
• Palm Springs Public Library. Archival issues of *Palm Springs Villager, Palm Springs Life,* and Palm Springs telephone directory. www.Accessingthepast.org
• *Desert Sun*, California Digital Newspaper Collection, a project of the Center for Bibliographical Studies and Research at the University of California, Riverside. https://cdnc.ucr.edu/cgi-bin/cdnc
• Clemson Agricultural College archive. tigerprints.clemson.edu
• Simon Elliott and Molly Haigh, Library Special Collections, Charles E. Young Research Library, UCLA. George R. Szanik photography archive.
• Special Collections, Getty Research Institute. John Lautner, Welton Becket, and Julius Shulman archives.
• Kathy Carbone, Institute Archivist, California Institute of the Arts, Chouinard Art Institute archive.
• David Glomb, who photographed *Palm Springs Modern* and picked up the thread for this book. Anthony Tam for permission to show the photography of Leland Y. Lee. Paula Taggart for sharing the photography of her late husband Fritz Taggart.

• Writer and architectural historian Melissa Riche, whose book *Mod Mirage: The Midcentury Architecture of Rancho Mirage* was recently published by Gibbs Smith.
• Steven M. Price, the author of *Trousdale Estates: Midcentury to Modern in Beverly Hills* (Regan Arts, 2017), who contributed a snappy take on the Eugene V. and Frances Klein House in Trousdale (see p. 116).
• Los Angeles designer Brad Dunning, a walking design encyclopedia and part of the wave of homebuyers who started restoring houses in Palm Springs in the mid-1990s.

To those who knew or worked with Arthur Elrod and who helped breathe life into this narrative:
• Arthur Elrod's nephew Michael Calloway, who provided family photographs and remembrances. Michael grew up in Easley, South Carolina, and visited Palm Springs several times between 1962 and 1971 to stay with Elrod and help out in the studio. He was the only family member Elrod took under his wing.
• Nelda Linsk, longtime Palm Springs resident, model, Realtor, co-owner with her late husband Joseph Linsk of Galerie du Jonelle, one-time owner of the Kaufmann House, client and close friend of Elrod's, and subject with her great friend Helen Dzo Dzo Kaptur of Slim Aaron's impeccably classic *Poolside Gossip* photograph, which freeze-frames Palm Springs at the pinnacle of midcentury chic.
• Mari Anne Pasqualetti, daughter of architect E. Stewart and Mari Williams. After she graduated from college with a degree in textile design and returned to Palm Springs, Mari went to work for Arthur Elrod. She started in January 1968 as an assistant to the newly hired Steve Chase just as the firm had moved into its new showroom. Mari worked there for two years until she took a job with an interior designer in San Francisco. She now resides in Arizona.
• Katherine Plake Hough, former chief curator of the Palm Springs Art Museum, who worked at Arthur Elrod Associates from 1973 to '75 as an assistant designer. She majored in

ACKNOWLEDGMENTS

interior architecture at California State University, Long Beach and was hired to take the thumbnail sketches of Arthur Elrod's and William Raiser's custom furnishings and develop them into large-scale drawings and details for cabinetmakers and upholsterers, as well as to create perspective drawings to show clients.

• Marybeth Norton Waterman, hired as a receptionist/administrative assistant in 1973/74. After Elrod's death, she worked for a design firm in Newport Beach, then moved back to Arthur Elrod Associates in 1976 as a project manager/assistant designer under the partnership of Steve Chase and Harold Broderick. She left with Steve Chase in 1980 when he formed his own company and worked with him through 1994. Upon his death, she became a partner in his ongoing company for eight years, then left to form her own company in 2002.

• Paige Rense-Noland, former editor in chief of *Architectural Digest*, now editor emeritus, who credits a handful of leading interior designers, Arthur Elrod among them, with helping her turn the magazine into an international powerhouse.

• Charles Hollis Jones, the renowned furniture designer, who met Arthur Elrod when he was a teenager working at Hudson-Rissman, the leading supplier of accessories to the design trade in Los Angeles. When Jones left to design his own acrylic and Lucite furnishings, Elrod was one of his first and best clients.

• Catherine Cody Nemirovsky, the youngest daughter of architect William F. Cody. She organized an exhibit on her father's work titled *Fast Forward: The Architecture of William F. Cody*, which debuted at the A+D Museum, Los Angeles, in 2016 and then traveled in 2017 to the Palm Springs Public Library. Cathy is working on a book about her father's complete body of work.

Palm Springs benefits from a tightly knit and very proactive network of organizations run by people who appreciate, support, and fight for historic architecture and design. These include the Palm Springs Modern Committee, Palm Springs Preservation Foundation, Palm Springs Historical Society, Palm Springs Historic Site Preservation Board, and the Racquet Club Estates Neighborhood Organization. My thanks in particular to Mark Davis, Gary Johns, Steven Keylon, Chris Menrad, Brian McGuire, and Robert Perry.

The many fellow architects and authors of John Lautner who over the years have helped raise his profile and place his work in the architectural pantheon, where he belongs: Helena Arahuete, Frank Escher, Alan Hess, the late Bette Jane Cohen, Mark Haddawy, and Judith Lautner, and the John Lautner Foundation.

The children and grandchildren whose families had homes designed by Elrod and to former and current homeowners: Debbie Hamling and Robert Ball, Philip and Margot Ittleson, Billy Steinberg, Keith and Jill Crosley, Jo Haldeman, Steve Maloney, Jan Weinstein, Michael Johnston, and David Zippel, and Rick Lord.

For their insight and input: Barbara Foster, Peter Wolf, Timothy Braseth, Trina Parks, Susan Secoy Jensen, Ron de Salvo, Sidney Williams, and Lauren Weiss Bricker.

And, finally, to my publisher, the late Gibbs Smith, who filled a much-needed niche in Palm Springs for books about Desert Modernism. I enjoyed our conversations, and his passion, intelligence, and curiosity about design will be greatly missed. It has been a pleasure to collaborate on this book with editor Katie Killebrew and book designer Kurt Wahlner.

Arthur Elrod was notoriously tight lipped about his childhood. He wasn't being deceptive. He simply never, ever talked about his family.

He merely did what countless others who leave the past in the past have done before him—he took the part of his upbringing that he disliked the most and rewrote it to suit his narrative. And he never looked back. By the mid-1960s his bio stated unequivocally that he was a native of Atlanta. The vagueness about his place of birth extended to his date of birth. His grave marker says simply 1923–74. Newspaper and magazine articles used 1924, 1925, or 1926 as their base of reference.

He was born Arthur Dea Elrod Jr. on August 8, 1924, the only child of Arthur Dea Elrod (1886–1941) and Jessie Herron Elrod (1888–1963), on a small farm on Flat Rock Road, Anderson, South Carolina.

He was close to his schoolteacher mother, Jessie; to his farmer father, not so much. After the influenza epidemic of 1918, the Elrods took in and adopted orphan Samuel Lee Calloway, who became Samuel Elrod Calloway, and raised him alongside their son.

Sam's son Michael Calloway says that his father and Arthur never got along. Sam, even though he was six years older and taller, resented having to do all the tougher farm chores and felt mistreated by Arthur Sr., while "Uncle A.D.," as Michael called Arthur Jr., was sheltered by his mother and never got his hands dirty.

Michael Calloway, who grew up 30 miles away in Easley, describes the Elrod farmhouse thus: "It was a simple brick house. It still has the big tree and dirt driveway we pulled in on when I was a kid to visit Grandma Jessie every Sunday. The driveway continued to the back, where there was a chicken house on the left, complete with brick furnace to mature the eggs. There were chickens everywhere in the back. On the right was a milk house for cows. I don't remember how much land they had, but most of it fell to the back right of the house. My father plowed it with a mule.

"On the far right end of the yard was a pear tree that looks like it's gone now. There was something about that lonely pear tree I liked. Jessie had plants and trees I had never seen before. There was a straw swing on the porch and cacti in pots she had brought from Palm Springs. Early on, Uncle A. D. flew her out there and had her visit. I still have one of her paintings of the mountains. She was quite a good painter. He bought her a Plymouth with push-button transmission on the dash—the latest thing then. We were amazed at Uncle A. D. But now you can see why he had to leave."

Arthur Elrod had no interest in being a farmer and was determined to put as much distance between himself and Flat Rock Road as possible. He started by going to the then all-male military school Clemson Agricultural College (now Clemson University), about 20 miles away in the foothills of the Blue Ridge Mountains, where the only options were to study animal husbandry and agriculture or textiles. Elrod chose textiles. Thanks to cotton, the textile industry in the South was a massive concern that employed hundreds of thousands, and Clemson was the first southern school to train textile specialists. It offered a well-regarded four-year course in its School of Textiles in textile engineering, textile chemistry and dyeing, and weaving and designing. Elrod enrolled as a sophomore in textile engineering for the 1942–43 academic year.

After one year at Clemson, he went to Atlanta to work at the city's leading upscale department store, Davisons, which was then owned by R. H. Macy & Co. His interest in textiles may have steered him to a job in the home furnishings department, a pattern he would repeat over the next 10 years. Atlanta was his first big-city experience. It's where he realized that in order to advance his career he would need to study interior design. And it's where he preferred to start his biography.

Around 1945 or '46, Elrod headed to Los Angeles to take an interior decoration course at the Chouinard Art

THE BEGINNING

A young Arthur Dea Elrod Jr. in a family photograph from the mid-1930s taken in front of the modest farmhouse on Flat Rock Road in Anderson, South Carolina, where he was raised.

Institute, an independent arts school at 743 Grand View near MacArthur Park. "I don't think he headed west because he knew anyone or had any family connections there," says his nephew Michael Calloway. "I think he wanted to get as far away as he could to a progressive place. He wasn't the least bit interested in the Elrod family, except for his mother. I'm amazed he kept the Elrod name."

Chouinard offered a professional four-year curriculum that included courses in fine art, advertising illustration, animation, costume design, and interior design. The emphasis was on teaching the practical side of the arts so that students would find employment directly after graduating, especially in the booming motion picture industry. Among the instructors were artist Millard Sheets, furniture designer Milo Baughman, and architect Thornton Abell. One classmate was Bob Winquist, who would become one of the most influential teachers of character animation at Chouinard and then the California Institute of the Arts. The interior decoration course was taught by Philip H. Pratt and included classes in interior architecture, space planning, estimating and reading blueprints along with field trips. This course description is from the 1943 catalog: "Living rooms, bedrooms, and dining rooms should be designed for those persons who will occupy them. A decorator must be able to discover the character of his client, adapt it to the purse, and season it with his own training and experience." Because of the war, the school offered abbreviated classes, including a six-week summer session, at a reduced rate.

PALM SPRINGS
PART ONE

1947—1952

E lrod could have spent a few weeks or a couple of years at Chouinard; it's difficult to know because no attendance records from the period exist. By 1947 he had departed Los Angeles for Palm Springs. And by this point he had taken elocution lessons to lose his southern accent. "He was always working on himself, always wanting to improve himself," says furniture designer Charles Hollis Jones. He may have tamed his accent, but he never lost that innate southern charm, and it would serve him in good stead throughout his career. Everyone who knew him remembers him as a true gentleman—always polite, always respectful, always gracious.

What was the allure of Palm Springs? From spending time in Los Angeles, he would have heard or read about how inviting this desert resort was. How all the movie stars and industrialists headed there during the season, from November through April, and how they were all building houses. What better way to improve himself than in an affluent resort town surrounded by wealth?

He rented an apartment at 470 Avenida Olancha and found a job as a junior staff decorator in the home furnishings department at the newly opened Bullock's Palm Springs. Until it moved to its location on Palm Canyon Drive in October 1947, Bullock's had operated a seasonal shop on the grounds of the Desert Inn. The store's new Streamline Moderne building by Wurdeman & Becket stood out for many reasons. Bullock's was the first full-scale department store in Palm Springs and featured the village's first elevator, which led up to the second-floor home furnishings department. It was a harbinger of other modern department stores that moved to Palm Canyon Drive—Robinson's, Saks Fifth Avenue, I. Magnin—that catered to an increasingly urbane, cosmopolitan clientele.

OPPOSITE: **In 1947 Elrod moved to Palm Springs where he worked as a junior decorator in the home department of the newly opened Bullock's department store.** RIGHT: **Elrod in his early 20s at the Chouinard Art Institute in Los Angeles.**

"The new store will be unique in its expression of desert living," architects Walter Wurdeman and Welton Becket told the *Desert Sun* (December 14, 1945). "The building is being planned so that a feeling of out-of-door freedom enters every major selling area. Glass walls from floor to ceiling will be bordered by flower and shrub gardens, while opaque walls will be of heat-resistant Thermopane faced with adobe and desert stone. The new store will include a home

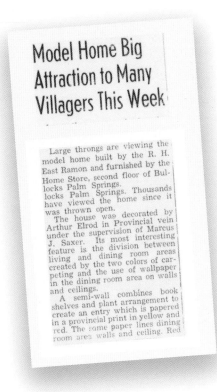

Model Home Big Attraction to Many Villagers This Week

Large throngs are viewing the model home built by the R. H. East Ramon and furnished by the Home Store, second floor of Bullocks Palm Springs. Thousands have viewed the home since it was thrown open.

The house was decorated by Arthur Elrod in Provincial vein under the supervision of Marcus J. Saxer. Its most interesting feature is the division between living and dining room areas created by the two colors of carpeting and the use of wallpaper in the dining room area on walls and ceilings.

A semi-wall combines book shelves and plant arrangement to create an entry which is papered in a provincial print in yellow and red. The same paper lines dining room area walls and ceiling. Red

furnishings studio, home accessories, and patio furniture units."

"In the 1940s, Bullock's was the only place in town to buy the bedding, furnishings, and accessories needed to furnish a home," says longtime Palm Springs resident Barbara Foster, whose home was designed by William Cody and furnished by Elrod. "It's where everyone went, and it's where he probably met a lot of clients who were shopping there." Bullock's was also the source that builders relied on to furnish their demonstration model homes around town.

It was an auspicious time to be in the home furnishings and interior design world. The postwar building boom that exploded on the West Coast took hold in the desert, where thousands of GIs had been stationed during World War II before flying out to North Africa or the Pacific. They flocked back needing reasonably priced homes for their families, and developers responded with large-scale housing tracts. Builders in the desert were also experimenting with new concepts in shared-amenity housing—cooperatives, condominiums, garden apartments, and mobile home parks—that were affordable and low maintenance for seasonal residents. The architects who would collectively influence the look of the village—John Porter Clark, Albert Frey, William F. Cody, E. Stewart Williams, Robson Chambers, Donald Wexler, Richard Harrison, Howard Lapham, Herbert Burns, Hugh Kaptur—were setting up shop and wading

into the conversation about the kind of building that was appropriate to the desert climate and to the changing tastes of the times.

There had been glimmers of architectural Modernism in the desert in the 1920s and '30s, including Rudolph Schindler's cabin in Coachella for Paul and Betty Popenoe (1922), Lloyd Wright's Oasis Hotel (1924), the Kocher-Samson building by A. Lawrence Kocher and Albert Frey (1934), Richard Neutra's Grace Lewis Miller House (1936), the John Porter Clark House (1939), and the Albert Frey House I (1940), among others. But until the late 1940s, the prevailing method of building in the desert remained the ancient way: adobe bricks, thick plaster walls, and small windows covered with shutters, all intended to block out the sun and keep interiors cool. The romanticized Spanish Colonial/Mexican hacienda, with its flourishes of red tile roofs, Saltillo tile floors, wood-beam ceilings, elaborate ironwork, and courtyards with fountains, was as popular in Palm Springs as the rest of Southern California.

One of the first mentions of Elrod's work in print came in 1948, when he decorated the interiors of a model home in the new Vista Del Cielo tract for local builder Bill Grant: "Large throngs are viewing the model home built by the R. H. Grant Construction Co. on East Ramon and furnished by the Home Store, second floor of Bullocks Palm Springs. Thousands have viewed the home since it was thrown open. . . . The house was decorated by Arthur Elrod in Provincial vein under the supervision of Marcus J. Saxer. Its most interesting feature is the division between living and dining room areas created by the two colors of carpeting and the use of wallpaper in the dining room area on walls and ceilings. . . . " (Editorial, *Desert Sun*, February 27, 1948).

Other mentions in the *Desert Sun* followed over the next few years:

New Villagers: Pennsylvanians Buy Palm Springs Home
Mr. and Mrs. Samuel Friedberg from Ambridge, Pa., have purchased a new home on Paseo de Anza and have engaged Bullock's ace decorator, Arthur Elrod, to do their interior decorating

and furnishings, which is attracting a great deal of attention among Palm Springs home owners.
      —Editorial, Desert Sun, *March 12, 1948*

Exclusive Listing: 1585 South Calle Marcus
This is an ideal home in every respect. On a corner lot in one of the substantial neighborhoods it has two bedrooms, each with its own bath and there's a den for an occasional guest. Large living room; large kitchen. Tastefully decorated by Arthur Elrod from the Bullock organization. $27,500. Robert Ransom Realtor
      —Advertisement, Desert Sun, *April 6, 1951*

By the late 1940s, the popular Spanish Colonial style was not just looking dated; it was also too costly to mass-produce. Builders were seeking home styles that they could construct at a reasonable cost and sell in volume. One solution was the sprawling one-story ranch house, with access to the outdoors from every room, which evolved as a modern version of the hacienda adapted to the postwar lifestyle. But no one was embracing Modern architecture en masse quite yet.

After six years in Palm Springs, Elrod was ready to broaden his knowledge. He moved to San Francisco in 1952 to work as a decorator at W. & J. Sloane, where he oversaw an exhibit at the San Francisco Museum of Art called Diamond Jubilee of Light. General Electric celebrated the 75th anniversary of Edison's incandescent light bulb with an installation of innovative lighting for modern interiors. BELOW: The exhibit was written up in the June 1954 issue of *Interior Design*, Elrod's first national coverage. OPPOSITE: Elrod (in his first professional headshot) titled his concept The Celestial Room since the room was lit for nighttime and used only artificial lighting precisely mapped out to match the furniture placement.

In 1952, Elrod left Bullock's Palm Springs and moved to San Francisco to join the renowned furnishings, interior design, and carpet emporium W. & J. Sloane.

In 1843, Scotsman William Sloane began selling rugs and importing Oriental carpets out of a storefront at Broadway and 19th Street in New York. Sloane was later joined by his younger brother John, and W. & J. Sloane established itself as the first home furnishings retailer in the United States, providing carpets, rugs, tapestries, and antiques for many major hotels and department stores, including the Waldorf Astoria, Plaza Hotel, and Holland House in New York. As the company grew, a branch was opened in Washington, DC to supply carpets to the White House.

In the 1870s, one of the Sloane brothers happened to be visiting San Francisco as the new Palace Hotel was under construction. He saw a business opportunity to provide carpets for what would become the city's preeminent luxury hotel, located at Market and New Montgomery Streets, and shortly thereafter W. & J. Sloane opened a store in San Francisco at 525 and 527 Market Street. Over the decades, the San Francisco branch of W. & J. Sloane expanded and moved several times, finally settling at 222 Sutter Street. Sloane's services had grown to include selling reproduction furniture and offering in-house interior decorating services. In the early 1940s, the company introduced modern furnishing lines, such as Baker and Widdicomb. In 1948, it announced the construction of a new Paul Williams–designed store at 9560 Wilshire Blvd. in Beverly Hills.

By the time Elrod arrived in 1952, W. & J. Sloane was well established as San Francisco's leading home store. His job as

SAN FRANCISCO

1952–1954

an interior decorator in the modern furnishings department gave him access to a wider range of decorating services and a broader client base in the residential as well as hospitality and commercial fields than his work at Bullock's had provided.

Again Elrod immediately attracted attention. A highly publicized installation opportunity for Elrod came when General Electric sought to demonstrate its latest lighting innovations for contemporary interiors and show how cost-effective they were. The company mounted its Diamond Jubilee of Light exhibit at the San Francisco Museum of Art from April 5 to May 11, 1954, to celebrate the 75th anniversary of the invention of Edison's incandescent

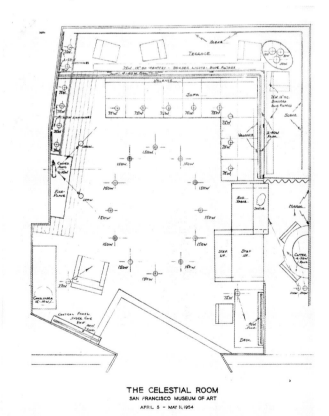

THE CELESTIAL ROOM
SAN FRANCISCO MUSEUM OF ART
APRIL 5 – MAY 11, 1954

light bulb. A portion of a penthouse complete with a living area, dining alcove and outdoor terrace was constructed inside the museum, with all the lighting provided by GE and all the furnishings by W. & J. Sloane. Elrod was selected as the room's designer.

Elrod called his concept the Celestial Room since it was intended as a nighttime experience using only artificial lighting with no floor or table lamps. All the furnishings, except for a custom sofa, were by the influential English designer T. H. Robsjohn-Gibbings. It was the first time his new line had been shown on the West Coast. Elrod meticulously matched the furniture and art placement with GE's highly technical lighting system, which included valance lighting around the perimeter of the living area; a downlight color constellation that changed color to suit the seasons, from warm summer evenings to cold foggy days; concealed dimmer-controlled spotlights in the dining alcove; concealed theatrical border lights with blue filters on the terrace that created a soft moonlight effect; and even dimmer-controlled, frosted flame–shaped lamps in the candelabra. It was the first use of recessed downlights in conjunction with fluorescents, and it marked the first appearance in Northern California of GE's electric fluorescent dimmer. As part of the exhibit, the museum sponsored a series of talks about residential lighting, and Elrod participated in a discussion on planning a room for light and color with Fred Durkee of Scalamandré and Barbara Wills, furniture buyer for Sloane.

The Celestial Room exercise stayed with Elrod his entire career—the importance of installing a complete, complex lighting system that went hand in hand with the placement of furniture and art to create an environment that functioned smoothly by day or night. In the June 1954 issue of *Interior Design*, the Celestial Room was given a full page of editorial coverage. Praise continued in the January 1955

Elrod's installation consisted of a penthouse with a living room, dining alcove, and outdoor terrace. Using white carpeting, pale blue ceiling, and brown fireplace wall, he placed custom sofas alongside T. H. Robsjohn-Gibbings's new line of furniture for Widdicomb. A complex lighting system—recessed downlights, valance lights, spotlights, hanging lamps—was controlled by dimmers while colored reflectors changed the mood.

By 1954 Elrod was eager to return to Palm Springs. He invited Harold C. (Hal) Broderick and Barbara Wills, whom he worked with at W. & J. Sloane, to join him in the newly formed Arthur Elrod Ltd., which would open as a "furniture and decorating business" at 886 N. Palm Canyon Drive in September 1954. OPPOSITE: Elrod's letter, dated July 6, 1954, and typed by Barbara Wills, to the *Desert Sun* inquiring about their advertising rates and advising of his new address.

issue of *House & Garden*. And in 1958, he was invited to GE's interior designers conference on lighting held at their lighting institute at Nela Park in Cleveland.

It was a watershed time in other ways. It was at W. & J. Sloane that Arthur Elrod met Harold C. Broderick. Born in Oakland, Hal Broderick received a degree in business administration from the University of Texas at Austin, attended the California College of Arts and Crafts, and graduated from the Rudolph Schaeffer School of Design in San Francisco. "I was going into advertising at the end of the war—to J. Walter Thompson—but the vets were returning," said Broderick in a 1996 interview. "So I worked at Sloane's in their business office, and after six weeks I knew everything I needed to know."

Arthur Elrod and Hal Broderick became business partners, an arrangement that would last until Elrod's death, and they were life partners until the mid-1960s. Elrod always took the lead in design, and Broderick assisted with interiors and took care of the business side. Arthur Elrod Ltd. was formed in San Francisco in 1954 using a temporary address at 468 Jackson St.; Elrod was then living at 2417 Webster St. They were joined by Barbara Wills, an assistant manager in Sloane's modern furniture department. Wills had started her design career at Cannell & Chaffin in Los Angeles, then moved to San Francisco to work at Macy's before joining Sloane's. She shared Elrod's affinity for all things contemporary. It was during these early years of Arthur Elrod Ltd. that Elrod established another habit that would continue throughout his entire career, becoming acquainted with local artists and sculptors and actively supporting them by collecting their works while they were still unknown.

A publicity release was sent to the *Palm Springs Villager* and

the Chamber of Commerce on July 1, 1954, announcing Elrod's return to the desert. On July 6, 1954, Elrod wrote to Palm Springs's *Desert Sun* newspaper, inquiring about their advertising rates. He also announced that he would be opening a Palm Springs showroom in September of that year, and that effective August 15, 1954, his new address would be 886 N. Palm Canyon Drive.

On July 7, 1954, the following announcement appeared in the trade newspaper *Retailing Daily*:

Elrod Leaves Sloane To Open Own Firm
San Francisco, July 7—
Arthur Elrod, decorator for W. & J. Sloane Co. has resigned to open his own decorating and furniture operation in Palm Springs, Cal. Associated with him in the store, to be known as Arthur Elrod, Ltd., will be Miss Barbara Wills, assistant manager of modern furniture at Sloane's, who has also resigned . . . Until the Palm Springs store, located at 886 North Palm Canyon Drive, is ready, the new firm will headquarter at 468 Jackson Street, San Francisco . . . Mr. Elrod had been with Bullock's, Palm Springs unit, until he joined Sloane's in 1952. Previously, Miss Wills was with Macy's San Francisco and Cannell & Chaffin, Los Angeles.

Arthur Elrod's second Palm Springs chapter was about to begin.

                    temporary address   ARTHUR ELROD LTD.
                                             468 Jackson Street
                                             San Francisco, Calif.
                                             July 6, 1954

THE DESERT SUN
Palm Springs, California

Dear Sirs:

In September, 1954, I plan to open a furniture and decorating
business to be located at 886 North Palm Canyon Drive, Palm
Springs, California.

I would appreciate your advising me of your advertising rates,
and other information in regard to your advertising policies.
I plan to maintain this temporary office in San Francisco until
August 15 - at which time I am moving to Palm Springs.

Thank you for your cooperation, and you might also make a note
to change the address on my personal subscription to your paper
from:

        Arthur Elrod
        2417 Webster Street
        San Francisco, California

to:

        Arthur Elrod
        886 North Palm Canyon Drive
        Palm Springs, California

effective August 15, 1954.

Thank you,

Yours truly,

Arthur Elrod

ADE:w

PALM SPRINGS PART TWO

"Arthur had met many wealthy people when he worked at Bullock's," says Barbara Foster, 75-year Palm Springs resident who was a fashion editor for the *Palm Springs Villager* and provided models such as Barbara Marx, Helen Dzo Dzo, and Nelda Linsk for the many fashion shows staged around town. "One of them had bankrolled him to open his own business."

"Lillian Schlothan, who owned the Pepper Tree Inn, called Arthur and told him that a designer who rented a space on 886 N. Palm Canyon Dr. had passed away and would he like to come take over the business," Hal Broderick related in a 2005 symposium at the Palm Springs Art Museum. "Arthur came to Palm Springs, looked it over and thought no way was he going to take over somebody else's business. And then he came back to San Francisco and talked to Barbara Wills and myself and said would we like to join him in forming Arthur Elrod Ltd., which it was at that time. We said yes, and we opened the first office in 1954."

In anticipation of the opening, a steady stream of ads and small editorial mentions started appearing in the *Desert Sun* newspaper:

Arthur Elrod begins a Complete Home Furnishing Service for the Palm Springs Area.
We would enjoy having you stop in to say Hello, anytime after September third. Arthur Elrod, Ltd., 886 North Palm Canyon Drive. Phone 2824
—*Advertisement*, Desert Sun, *September 2, 1954*

Decorator Back in Palm Springs
One of the bright new shops opening in the Village this month is Arthur Elrod Ltd., which offers a complete home furnishings service for the Palm Springs area. Arthur Elrod, who returns to Palm Springs from San Francisco where he won fresh recognition for his decorating genius, is greeting old friends at 886 North Palm Canyon Drive.
—*Editorial*, Desert Sun, *September 9, 1954*

Elrod already knew the village's pioneering families—McManus, Hicks, Nichols, Bennett—so when he returned, it was a triumphant return, with many personal and social contacts already established. He was 30 years old.

Initially it was just the three of them—Elrod as the lead designer, Broderick as the business manager, and Wills as the showroom manager. More designers were hired as the firm expanded—Robert Blanks from Seattle in 1955, Robert W. Alexander and Helen Allyn Munkacsy in 1956, Emerson Whipple from W. & J. Sloane in San Francisco and artist Reg Acker as Elrod's personal assistant in 1957. The showroom stayed open year-round and usually completed projects over the summer while homeowners were away.

Thanks to their contacts from W. & J. Sloane, Arthur Elrod Ltd. brought nationally known furniture lines—Baker and Widdicomb—to the desert for the first time. Elrod made it clear in a press release he wrote for the Palm Springs Chamber of Commerce that he was focusing on a contemporary desert-appropriate look with his first collections—an exclusive display of T. H. Robsjohn-Gibbings's furniture and a line of Thaibok Fabrics Ltd. silks.

Arthur Elrod Ltd. was in immediate demand. Having a storefront presence on Palm Canyon Drive, which was part design studio and part furniture and fabric showroom, gave them instant visibility and credibility. Everyone driving into town would see the window displays that showed the furnishings and fabrics they provided, and they could stop in to purchase an accessory or hire the firm to furnish a vacation

Elrod benefited from close friendships with wealthy women, among them Mabel Schamberg in Chicago and Elsie Peiser Bond in San Francisco, who helped finance his business. OPPOSITE: Entry hall of the Hadley Stuarts's house in Idaho (see p. 174). "Arthur was totally original," said Hal Broderick. "His work was fresh, contemporary, innovative. And he took the look of the desert all over the country."

One of the firm's first jobs was arranging the T. H. Robsjohn-Gibbings furniture that Widdicomb, the furniture manufacturer, had donated to Lucille Ball and Desi Arnaz for their new house at Thunderbird Country Club in Rancho Mirage. Designed by architect Paul R. Williams, the single-level, 4,400-square-foot ranch house had six bedrooms and six bathrooms and overlooked the 9th and 18th fairways.

home, on short notice. An excellent testimonial appeared in the *Desert Sun* on August 4, 1955: "Last February H.C. Berkowitz visited the Village and stayed at Howard Manor. While here, he noticed Elrod's attractive furniture store on North Palm Canyon Drive, and decided that the shop exemplified a polished kind of decorating, and that Elrod should be the decorator for the Berkowitz vacation ranch in Wendell [Idaho]."

It's not surprising that the firm not only hit the ground running immediately upon opening, but that its first commissions were for Hollywood royalty. "We were the official reps for Widdicomb Furniture and Baker," Hal Broderick related. "Widdicomb called one day and said they had donated a house full of furniture designed by Robsjohn-Gibbings to a couple at Thunderbird Country Club and would we please go out and arrange it. Thus started our longtime relationship with Lucy and Desi Arnaz."

In 1954, Lucille Ball and Desi Arnaz had completed an early home at the newly opened Thunderbird Country Club in Rancho Mirage, which had transitioned in the early 1950s from a dude ranch with homey chuck wagon dinners and hayrides to a gated golf club with housing built along the fairways and a revamped clubhouse by William F. Cody. Their vacation home was designed by Paul R. Williams, the African American architect whose elegant residences were clustered around Los Angeles. He had designed W. & J. Sloane's new store in Beverly Hills, and had collaborated with A. Quincy Jones in Palm Springs on additions and renovations to the Tennis Club in 1947 and the Town & Country Center in 1948. Williams provided Ball and Arnaz with a low-slung, single-level, 4,400-square-foot ranch house with six bedrooms, six bathrooms, and a pool overlooking the 9th and 18th fairways.

A year later, Elrod was decorating Lucy and Desi's home at 1000 N. Roxbury Drive in Beverly Hills. "Arthur was called by Lucy to do over their house," said Broderick. "She had some problems with the Van Luit scenic wallpaper that

OPPOSITE: Elrod lightened the stone walls in Lucy and Desi's living room with a sinuous coffee table, sofas, end tables with straight legs, and modern lamps. Wall-to-wall carpets and fireplaces were common in the desert because most people vacationed there from November through April when evenings were cooler. LEFT: Double beds in the master overlooking the pool. BELOW: Variety of wicker and iron furniture for casual dining and lounging outdoors.

ran up the staircase. She called shortly after they moved in and screamed over the phone, 'Get those goddamn birds out of my house!' The copper pipes had burst and flooded the lower white-carpeted floor, and she felt the birds were the culprit. One of our staff got out her easel and paints, and soon the offending birds became beautiful butterflies. Lucy was an ardent fan of Arthur's and always remembered his birthday, which was close to hers."

Their next high-profile client was composer/pianist/singer Hoagy Carmichael, who was segueing from part-time visitor to full-time resident at Thunderbird Country Club and wanted to remodel and expand his house.

Around this time, showroom manager Barbara Wills decided to go out on her own. She announced in April 1956 that she was setting up her own interior design studio in the Sunset Tower building at 1078 N. Palm Canyon Drive. Her business partner and the president of Barbara Wills Inc. was . . . Hoagy Carmichael. Wills also listed an extensive selection of the same furnishings and fabric lines that were carried at Arthur Elrod Ltd. Unfortunately, hers was a short-lived enterprise. In 1959 she got married and settled in Grand Rapids, Michigan.

Even Elrod's former employer W. & J. Sloane announced in an ad on December 12, 1958 ("Oh Sunny Day! We've Arrived in Palm Springs!") that it too had opened a branch in Palm Springs, initially at 1078 N. Palm Canyon Drive in the same location as Barbara Wills's showroom, and then in 1964 moving to a larger location at 460 S. Palm Canyon Drive. Everyone was chasing the building boom in the desert, and everyone in the furnishings business wanted a piece of the action.

The fever extended to Hollywood. In 1955 actor Alan Ladd partnered with high school friend Bill Higgins to open a hardware and gift store at 533 S. Palm Canyon Drive. Claudette Colbert opened a boutique and art gallery, later occupied by Jolie Gabor's jewelry salon. Eva Gabor would open an interior design studio and furnish a model condo unit

at Rimcrest alongside one by Elrod. Celebrities-as-business owners only added to the chic mystique that was building around Palm Springs.

On February 15, 1956, the following announcement appeared in the *Desert Sun*: "Arthur Elrod was notified by the National Board of Governors of the American Institute of Decorators that he has been elected a member of the Southern California chapter of the AID. He is the only decorator in Palm Springs to be so honored. Presentation of the scroll was made last night at a banquet at the Tally Ho restaurant in Los Angeles. Among the homes Elrod has been in charge of decorating in the Village are those owned by Frank Bennett, Leon J. Koerner, Phillip Lyon, Mary Hurrell, Hoagy Carmichael, and Desi and Lucy Arnaz." These connections and friendships with the leaders of Palm Springs society were of paramount importance in helping Elrod solidify his status as the go-to designer in the desert.

Like many interior designers, Elrod and Broderick treated their homes as their laboratories and their calling cards. They each bought a series of houses, primarily in the Movie Colony, Racquet Club Road Estates, and Old Las Palmas neighborhoods, renovated them, decorated them, lived in some, sold them fully furnished, and moved on to the next project.

The first house that Elrod owned was a small Spanish adobe at 419 Valmonte Sur in the Movie Colony, which he bought from Frank and Melba Bennett in 1955. In the 1930s and '40s the Bennetts managed and then co-owned, with Dorothy and Philip Boyd, the popular Deep Well Guest Ranch, one of the first dude ranches in Palm Springs, which had been remodeled by architect Paul Williams. Dude ranches appealed to visitors wanting to tap into their inner cowboy; guests were encouraged to dress in western wear, and activities centered on horseback rides into the desert, barbecues, and campfires. "It wasn't very dude-y. It was more like a resort hotel," noted Phil Boyd, who served as Palm Springs's first mayor.

The Bennetts were actively involved in every aspect of the village's social and civic life. They were original members of the Desert Riders and they helped establish many of the village's most beloved traditions, including the Desert Circus and the Desert Classic Ball. Melba Bennett, one of the town's grande dames, was founder and president of the Palm Springs Historical Society, served on the board of directors of the Palm Springs Desert Museum, and volunteered for numerous charitable organizations. As an admirer of Robinson Jeffers, she wrote a biography of the poet titled *The Stone Mason of Tor House.*

Broderick had one very profound influence on Elrod: he introduced him to Christian Science. Elrod had been raised a Southern Baptist but he gravitated to Christian Science, which bases its beliefs in the power of healing sin and illness through prayer and faith. Both men became readers in the First Church of Christ, Scientist, Palm Springs, and were involved in the renovation of the church at 605 S. Riverside Drive, which was designed in 1956 by Albert Frey and Robson Chambers, and of the Christian Science Reading Room at 373 S. Palm Canyon Drive. An article in the January 21, 1956 *Desert Sun* described the look of the Reading Room:

> *The new Reading Room accommodates more visitors than previously, and is most attractive in appointments. The decorating was done by Arthur Elrod, interior decorator of prominence in Palm Springs. There are complete new furnishings, including drapes, carpeting, and dark walnut desks and chairs. Hemp grasscloth is used on the walls, while the color harmony of brown, aqua and beige lends a beauty of appearance and restfulness for study.*

Elrod's nephew Michael Calloway remembers driving from Palm Springs to Los Angeles with Elrod and Broderick while they read aloud from Christian Science founder Mary Baker Eddy's writings. And although Elrod later strayed from the church, he adhered to its basic tenets. "I've never been

to a doctor in my life, even when I broke my foot. I firmly believe that the mind controls all," he told Bea Miller (*Los Angeles Times Home*, March 15, 1970).

Elrod returned home to Anderson, South Carolina, once or twice in the late 1950s for the Christmas holidays. He hired local workers to renovate the family farmhouse with a modern bathroom and kitchen, and later he had the entire interior redone, complete with wall-to-wall carpeting, furniture, and lighting. Michael Calloway worshipped his uncle and he remembers how excited he got when his mother would tell him Uncle A. D. was in town. But when Elrod's mother, Jessie, became ill, Elrod didn't go to see her. And when she passed away in 1963, he attended her funeral but never set foot in Anderson or South Carolina again.

Elrod occasionally returned home for the holidays, and he had the family farmhouse renovated for his mother, Jessie. But after she passed away in 1963, he never set foot in South Carolina again.

THE
1950s

PREVIOUS PAGES: Ernest and Leonore Alschuler House (see p. 40). While Arthur Elrod pushed ahead with a modern agenda, many of his clients still preferred the familiarity of the traditional French Provincial look. BELOW: The first project he tackled for longtime clients Laurena Heple and Walt Bratney was their Pebble Beach home, published in the *Los Angeles Times Home* magazine on December 28, 1958. OPPOSITE: For the den, Elrod reupholstered existing sofas and chairs in his favorite peacock blue. Tailor-made shutters by Anna Mae Devereux replaced drapes.

1950s Design Evolution

The prevailing high style in interiors of the 1940s and '50s was French Provincial. It was a move away from the city look of stately fine French furniture toward the rustic country houses of Provence by way of New England. It involved acres of knotty pine or pecky cypress wall paneling, braided wool rugs, Windsor chairs around oak pedestal tables, pine hutches, big brass hinges and drawer pulls, yards and yards of red and green fabric, preferably in plaids, curtains that always matched the chair cushions, and quilted floral bedspreads on dual beds with matching drapes. It was a familiar, homey style for people who weren't ready to give up the family heirlooms.

Because his clients still clung to their mahogany dining sets, Elrod's interiors of the 1950s straddled the divide between traditional and contemporary. His work on Walter Bratney and Laurena Heple's Pebble Beach house was featured in the *Los Angeles Times Home* magazine: "Instead of discarding antiques, he refinished and reupholstered them, adding new pieces as needed" (December 28, 1958). But the technology, especially in kitchens, and the music and lighting systems were always advanced. As the *Desert Sun* noted in 1955 about Frank and Melba Bennett's house El

Sueno on Camino Mirasol, "It is a fine older home recently redecorated by Arthur Elrod, famous decorator in Palm Springs area, incorporating heirloom pine pieces, mementoes of world travels and the latest in push button living." This comfortable look suited his more conservative clients and was particularly suited to the low-key, low-profile environs of Smoke Tree Ranch, where he did interiors for Walt and Lillian Disney, Paul and Pearl Helms, George Murphy, Donald and Genevieve Gilmore, Harry and Katherine (Bud and Betty) Haldeman, and Arthur and I'Lee Bailey, as well as a spec home for himself.

Elrod pushed ahead with lighter colors, balanced antiques with contemporary sofas and light fixtures, and replaced heavy curtains with silk drapes or shutters, somehow forging a happy marriage between French Provincial and Robsjohn-Gibbings furniture. One of the only designers he ever named as inspiration was William Pahlmann, who was known for combining pieces from different periods. "So what's wrong with putting a Persian lamp on a Danish Modern table," Elrod said to *Los Angeles Times* columnist Joan Winchell (March 20, 1960). He also made sure that rooms served multiple functions: he enclosed porches to turn

them into usable lanais and converted seldom-used dining rooms into game rooms or studies. Above all, he respected quality, regardless of its age:

Arthur Elrod this week returned to Wendell, Idaho, where he is in exclusive charge of decorating the ranch home of H. C. Berkowitz, president of Old Mr. Boston Distillers . . . Deciding to plan the interior of the house in a French style, Elrod arranged to meet Berkowitz in New York. Most of the furniture selected has been fashioned of fine walnuts and fruitwoods, and every finish a special hand-rubbed one. The fabrics used for the upholstery and draperies are all of pure silk, some moirés, some taffeta-types, and some damasks. Because of the fine textures and tones of the wood pieces, the color planning has been

made very simple. The living area, for example is fashioned of blues and whites only that the wood tones may be brought into important focus.

—Desert Sun, *August 4, 1955*

In 1958, Ann Peppers, Thoroughbred horse breeder, philanthropist, and widow of Western Fruit Growers owner Tom Peppers, hired Elrod to renovate her Heather Downs ranch near Redlands, California. His response was a color scheme of brilliant emerald green and white. "Ann Peppers' home had the advantages of lovely views, comfortable location and spacious rooms but it was drab, some of the furnishings were dated and it lacked a distinctive quality. A seldom-used porch was transformed into a gay lanai with a

OPPOSITE: Since playing cards was a major social activity, a seldom-used dining room was converted into a game room and study. All things Oriental had become a major influence on interiors; a six-panel folding screen was turned into cupboard doors. BELOW: Elrod added a new hospitality room that served as a dining area with slate floors, a Chinese gold-leaf screen over a white damask sofa, and blue and green tasseled silk pillows stacked on the floor as extra seating.

bright colorful striped canvas ceiling, which gives the feeling of a Mediterranean villa. The Elrod craftsmen finished the living room and adjoining rooms in white with rich emerald green for color and adding touches of gold and the natural colors of the accent pieces. In the lanai, the creamy terrazzo has accents of green bottle glass for a very unique floor covering. The furniture throughout is principally French Provincial with some contemporary pieces" (*Redlands Daily Facts*, April 10, 1959).

Slowly but surely the postwar lifestyle shift from formal to informal had a direct impact on the way homes were being built and furnished. As houses moved into a lighter, more open mode, the traditional style started to look dated, clunky, and the wrong scale for homes that were expanding to accommodate young families. As entertaining at home became more commonplace, people wanted the flexibility

of an open floor plan that could accommodate bridge parties for 4 to 8 or dinner parties for 10 to 20, or cocktail parties for a crowd.

In the desert it was easy to turn this vision of a relaxed lifestyle into reality. Architects pushed developers to experiment with open-plan, post-and-beam homes that would be more suited to the desert climate. Instead of chopped up warrens of rooms, narrow galley kitchens, and stuffy unused dining rooms, the main living spaces opened to the pool and the views. Seemingly overnight the design had pivoted away from Spanish Colonial to Desert Modern or Ranch houses, as developers found that these affordable, low-maintenance styles sold very well. The colors of the desert led to a new palette for interiors—the soft color of the sand, the desert rose of the mountains, the sage greens of the foliage.

Elrod ignored those pastels, as well as the prevailing desert monotones of brown, beige, and tan in favor of his preferred foundation of white, which he then accented with a full spectrum of blues, greens, and yellows tied together with textured wallpapers and fabrics. Walnut became the preferred wood. Walls and floors were bleached, pickled, sandblasted, or stained. Every square inch of every room received attention. Every press write-up emphasized how fresh and energizing both he and his interiors were. "Arthur Elrod Has Brought Life to Desert Designing," proclaimed the *Desert Sun* in the first in-depth portrait of Elrod on January 10, 1956:

> *There's a young man in town—a handsome and most eligible bachelor—who can figuratively take the color of your eyes, the personality that is you—and blend these into a harmonious environment that is pleasing and definitely flattering. "My basic color is white because it has no color. I then use color in contrast to reflect the personality and individual desires of the homeowner and I keep the woman of the house constantly in mind. Wherever she may be in her home, colors must flatter and reflect her personality."*

Marilyn Hoffman in the *Christian Science Monitor* described his "special brand of decorating" as "airy, spacious, contemporary, and full of brilliant color and comfortable fabrics. . . . 'The desert fosters informal living—living geared to fabrics you can sit on in shorts and not get scratched,' [Elrod] said with a grin. Cobalt blue and lemon yellow have been a favorite color combination along with the more recent white-and-blue for bedrooms. Since lots of glass and sun make fading a problem, he uses no damasks. 'Linen is the most wonderful fabric for us.' " (September 2, 1959.)

Pierced wood or concrete grilles (patterned room dividers) replaced solid walls and delineated the barriers between entry and living room, living and dining room, or living room and sunken bar, with geometric patterns that

A corner of the Disneys' living room. Elrod's refreshing look for desert homes was described as "airy, spacious, contemporary, and full of brilliant color and comfortable fabrics." He would take the antique wood bracket shelf and adapt it as a modern floating console in his first home on Valmonte Sur (see p. 47).

simultaneously revealed and concealed. Kitchens were still placed at the back of the house and were still behind doors that now swung open, but the space was much larger and usually included a breakfast room, butler's pantry, desk and telephone, laundry area, and direct access to the garage. Elrod incorporated every new appliance and gadget into his kitchens, from the large (ranges and wall ovens, barbecues, refrigerators with ice makers, freezers, washers, and dryers) to the small (can openers, coffee makers, toasters, juicers, food mixers, trash compactors), and brought in kitchen designers for his larger projects.

A handful of houses that Elrod decorated in the mid-'50s exhibited the prevailing vogue for all things Oriental, thanks to the GIs who had been stationed in Asia and the Pacific during World War II and to increased air travel to Hawaii and Japan. Clients were amassing Far Eastern art and antiques along with casual rattan furniture, and both needed appropriate backdrops. The look became a mishmash of Japanese, Chinese, Hawaiian, and Polynesian influences, introducing teak furniture, scenic floral wallpapers, blue-and-white ceramics, folding lacquered screens, garden pagodas, and lanais to postwar designs. It also introduced paints and fabrics in celadon, gold, and spice colors with names such as Siamese Pine, Obi Orange, and Ming Yellow.

A 1,200-square-foot house in Deepwell Estates by architects Wexler & Harrison, which Elrod decorated in 1955 for Realtor William Boggess, showcased the new Japanese

Modern look. It featured a black, white, and Obi Orange color scheme, Chester "Cactus Slim" Moorten's use of crushed rock raked in the traditional Japanese manner for the landscaping, and an antique brass gong at the garden gate.

ED AND BERTHA ROBBIN HOUSE

1120 Alejo Road, Ruth Hardy Park

A house for Ed and Bertha Robbin, built in 1948 by architectural designer Herbert Burns, with interiors updated by Elrod in 1956, blended the Oriental with the desert. It featured celadon green carpet, gold textured fabric on a semicircular sofa, scenic wallpaper of a flowering tree, a black lacquered buffet, a teak dining table, grasscloth-covered walls, and handwoven drapes in matchstick bamboo with metallic threads. It was modern yet understated, comfortable yet colorful. Thomas and Lynn Starr Hull's home in Deepwell, built by Sam Pascal, was also done in an Oriental decorating scheme and was featured as the House of the Year in the June/July 1960 issue of *Palm Springs Life*.

ABOVE: **A 1948 house by architectural designer Herbert Burns was updated by Elrod in 1956 for Ed and Bertha Robbin and was published in the *Palm Springs Villager*, September 1956. Olive, bottlebrush, palm, and lemon trees and over 27 varieties of cactus were planted by landscape architect Martin Ruderman.** RIGHT: **Bertha Robbin's interest in Chinese culture was reflected in the furnishings and colors—davenport (as sofas were called) upholstered in soft gold fabric, handwoven drapes of matchstick bamboo with metallic threads, lamps made from Chinese vases, celadon carpets, and teak tables.**

ERNEST AND LEONORE ALSCHULER HOUSE

425 Via Lola, Old Las Palmas

Ernest and Leonore (Lee) Alschuler, who divided their time between Chicago and Palm Springs and were heavily involved in community events and fund-raising, built an understated house at 425 Via Lola with architect Howard Lapham and structural engineer Kenneth Iwata. Modeled on a Japanese country house, the home's materials were adapted to the climate: the roof had handmade concrete shingles, instead of wood, cut in an Oriental pattern, and the garage doors were of aluminum faced with reeds. Elrod left the terrazzo floors bare in keeping with the restrained feel and carefully arranged the couple's collections of Japanese antiques and art. "The fountain courtyard featured olive trees trimmed like ming trees and a lanai that faced a garden where a fountain splashes into a pool" (*Desert Sun*, February 14, 1961). Lee Alschuler was a keen gardener and president of the Palm Springs Garden Club. She and Elrod won Best Lighted Tree Shrubbery awards in the village's annual Let There Be Light Christmas contest in 1963 for their Via Lola and Valmonte Sur homes, respectively.

The Alschulers sold their house to financier Henry Ittleson Jr. and his wife, Nancy, who brought Elrod in to transform the Japanese look into a chrome and stainless steel Modernist oasis with custom furnishings. "My grandfather was color blind, but he could see yellow," said Philip Ittleson, who has many of his grandparents' custom Elrod furnishings. "So Elrod used a tremendous amount of yellow in their homes." The Ittlesons, who hired Elrod to furnish their New York apartment at The Pierre and their villa Rien Ne Va Plus in the south of France, in turn sold the furnished house to Sidney and Alexandra Sheldon.

OPPOSITE: Ernest and Lee Alschuler asked architect Howard Lapham and engineer Kenneth Iwata to create a *minka*, a Japanese farmhouse adapted to the desert climate with handmade concrete roof shingles instead of wood and aluminum garage doors faced with reeds. LEFT: Hand-adzed torii doors led into a courtyard with a garden pagoda. Shoji screens opened to the living area. Elrod kept the terrazzo floors bare and the furnishings to a minimum. BELOW: All the furniture in the carpeted master bedroom had an Oriental motif, from the lacquered fretwork headboard to the chairs, pair of low tables, and black-and-white Japanese prints.

BELOW: A pair of rattan peacock chairs in the informal garden lanai/ study that overlooked the pool. OPPOSITE: The back terrace had overscale wood outdoor furniture upholstered in acacia yellow, another Elrod signature color. Steps led down to the freeform pool set against a backdrop of the San Jacinto Mountains.

ARTHUR ELROD HOUSE I

419 Valmonte Sur, Movie Colony

Elrod received a building permit for a $2,000 remodel of his house at 419 Valmonte Sur on November 15, 1958, and another for a $5,000 addition on August 22, 1959. The lengthy renovation literally raised the roof of the small old adobe and opened it to the desert views. The house was featured on January 29, 1961, in the *Los Angeles Times Home* magazine, billed as "A Dramatic Transformation." The modern silhouette that emerged was slender and vertical, achieved by raising ceiling heights from 8 to 12 feet, and adding tall windows with floor-to-ceiling shutters, a floor-to-ceiling concave brick fireplace wall between the living and dining rooms, and walls of sliding glass doors that opened to a covered outdoor patio and lanai. Elongated front doors became a thing, in this case amplified by Elrod's use of long door pulls and flanked by a distinctive pair of antique figurine sconces. The interiors deftly blended antiques with contemporary art, rugs, and lighting. Elrod would sell the house to actor Laurence Harvey and his second wife, Joan Cohn, widow of Hollywood film mogul Harry Cohn.

TOP: Elrod's first house started as a small adobe. LEFT: An ink wash of the lanai shows the egg-crate top trimmed with canvas, trelliswork, and tie-back drapes. ABOVE: One side of the living room moved to a contemporary beat, with a rug woven in raised multicolored patterns, an abstract painting, white furniture, and floor-to-ceiling shutters. OPPOSITE: After an overhaul, the elegant house that emerged accentuated height with 12-foot ceilings and light with plenty of windows. Tall double front doors were flanked by a pair of figural sconces.

OPPOSITE: A concave off-white brick wall separated the living room from the dining room.
BELOW: Valmonte Sur was Elrod's first lab where he could experiment with customized furniture, starting in the entry, which had yellow canvas drapes and a black tile floor, with a floating console shelf on brackets. European antiques still linger on the right side of the living room—ornate carved mirror, glass girandoles, and a pair of Louis XVI-style armchairs.

THEODORE AND MARGUERITE SUTTER HOUSE

1207 Calle de Maria, Deepwell Estates

One of Elrod's early projects, the Sutter Residence at 1207 Calle de Maria, showed how he could complement E. Stewart Williams's exacting architecture. Because Williams was such a master of materials and because he included finishing details down to the mailbox as part of his design scheme, the Sutter interiors required only the most basic furnishings—sofas and end tables, a dining table and chairs, beds, lamps, rugs, and drapes as needed. Elrod provided restrained pieces by Widdicomb that didn't outshine the structure. All shelves and bookcases were built-ins. Texture was provided by wood paneling, patterned cabinet doors, an exterior concrete block screen and steel trellis, and milk glass windows by the entry.

BELOW: The front façade of the Sutter house in Deepwell by architect E. Stewart Williams was a precise procession of concrete blocks and milk glass, which created a privacy screen for the entryway. Extensive built-ins and cabinetry designed by Williams meant that Elrod only had to provide the basics, and he chose his go-to furniture line, T. H. Robsjohn-Gibbings's furnishings for Widdicomb. "Gibby," a favorite of both men, had worked with Williams on a project in Texas and with Elrod on Tom and Dottie Davis's fantasy palace in Thunderbird Heights.

TOP: The living room flowed out to the pool terrace, which was shaded by a steel grid trellis. ABOVE: Views of the living and dining areas. "My dad had great respect for Arthur's work," says Mari Anne Pasqualetti, E. Stewart Williams's daughter, who worked for Elrod. "And he had a lovely friendship with Gibby."

There were other interior designers practicing in the desert, locals like Noel Birns, Antone Dalu, Joan Billings, Gary Jon, and Vee Nisley. And there were designers from Los Angeles who did second homes for their clients, such as Harold Grieve (Lily Pons, Bing Crosby), Catherine Armstrong (her own desert house), and Helen Conway (Earle and Marion Jorgensen, Jerome J. Robinson), as well as the big firms Cannell & Chaffin and W. & J. Sloane. That was the way things usually worked—designers did the principal residence and were then asked to tackle the vacation home.

But a funny thing happened with Elrod. People would hire him first for their desert vacation homes and then ask him to work on their main houses around the country. "Arthur worked in reverse," said Paige Rense-Noland, editor emeritus and former editor in chief of *Architectural Digest*. "He was the one who persuaded clients to look at their second or third house on a par with their primary residence. He made clients want to spend money on their weekend houses."

Elrod stood apart in other ways, mainly in his embrace of the new, his willingness to experiment, and his curiosity about innovative technology, fabrication techniques, and materials. These qualities endeared him to the Modernist architects he worked with over the course of his career, a stellar group that included E. Stewart Williams, William F. Cody, Buff & Hensman, A. Quincy Jones, Wexler & Harrison, Palmer & Krisel, Howard Lapham, Hugh Kaptur, Richard Dorman, Edward Fickett, and John Lautner.

John Porter Clark's 1939 house for Alice Guthrie on Via Miraleste in the Movie Colony was purchased in 1955 by Edwin H. "Buddy" Morris, a hugely successful music publisher and ASCAP board member, and his wife, Carolyn. Elrod's renovations to the house were featured in the *Palm Springs Villager*, showcasing the Morrises' collection of antiques and Impressionist art set against white oak floors in the living areas and deep-pile white carpeting in the bedrooms. This would be the first of seven homes Elrod would complete for Morris, a record for the number of projects commissioned by one client.

Joseph Pawling was a local builder who enjoyed designing houses that featured what he called "creative building ideas." He gave architects Donald Wexler and Richard Harrison one of their first custom residential commissions after they left William F. Cody's office and opened their own practice: two neighboring glass, stone, and steel homes at 230 and 231 Lilliana Drive in the Mesa, built in 1954/1955. The butterfly-roof house at 231 Lilliana, which was Joe and Joyce Pawlings' own home, was decorated by Elrod in oleander red, yellow, black, and sand tones. The house had two features that were becoming popular: it wrapped around an open central garden atrium, and it featured a pool patio, a shade-covered, partially enclosed area between the living room and the pool.

Elrod worked again with Wexler & Harrison in 1957 on the Sydney and Rachel Charney House at Tamarisk Country Club, three model homes for Calcor/Rheem's prefabricated Steel Development Houses in 1962, the model units of

Royal Air Country Club Apartments on Tahquitz Drive, and the Martin Anthony Sinatra Medical Education Center at the Desert Hospital. And he worked with E. Stewart Williams on assorted projects over the years, including the Koerner House and the new Palm Springs Desert Museum.

But his most notable relationship was with Palm Springs's maverick architect William F. Cody. Their collaboration started modestly in the mid-1950s with Elrod providing furnishings for Cody's own family home at 1950 E. Desert Palms Drive. Cody's youngest daughter, Catherine Cody Nemirovsky, recalls the living room arrangement, which had to be customized to fit around the sunken conversation pit: "Elrod provided the two davenports—as my father always called the sofas—in hues of dark blue, purple, and black tweed with simple straight chrome legs and four matching elongated cushions around the top edge of the conversation pit. There were two white laminated-top tables with black spindly legs around the pit and a black Formica inlaid teak cocktail table and matching corner table. Elrod also modified a giant German beer stein, which had been a wedding gift, into a lamp that sat on the corner table between the davenport and the two-seater."

Cody and Elrod worked on a Mexican-style house on La Mirada in 1968 for contractor and Palm Springs mayor William Foster and his wife, Barbara, who still lives there. Their design innovations included electronic curtains outside the master bedroom window, a built-in lava stone barbecue in the kitchen, and a trash chute that went from the kitchen to the basement. They also collaborated on an addition to Richard Neutra's Kaufmann House for Joseph and Nelda Linsk, numerous custom homes, and most memorably, the Eldorado Country Club Clubhouse.

Every write-up of Elrod in the local *Desert Sun* newspaper mentioned the energy and vitality he brought to the desert as well as the fact that he was a young, charming bachelor. Everyone who knew Elrod, worked for him, or was a client remarked on his charm, enthusiasm, and intense work ethic. His salesmanship skills were already legendary. These mentions in the *Desert Sun* sum up his standing in the community: "This 31-year-old native of the Deep South started with practically nothing in this town two years ago but to illustrate the terrific impact he has made upon home owners in the Palm Springs resort area, this past year his gross sales in furniture and services have amounted to more than $300,000. . . . He is a busy young man with a staff of eight plus seven more in his custom drapery department . . ." (January 10, 1956). "Two things strike you when you meet Elrod for the first time: his youth, for you are somehow expecting him to be a much older man; and the calmness with which he goes about his work" (February 6, 1962).

By June 1956, just less than two years after it opened, the showroom had doubled in size and been redecorated in gold and white. Elrod continued to expand the furniture lines, many of which, like Paul McCobb's Linear Group, were being introduced to the desert for the first time. Elrod opened the studio to artists and artisans he supported and

Elrod's collaboration with architect William F. Cody began with some furnishings for Cody's living room. Elrod provided the davenport (as Cody called the sofa) and matching two-seater upholstered in dark blue, purple, and black tweed; black Formica inlaid teak cocktail table and matching corner table; and white Formica inlaid tables for the sunken conversation pit. He also turned the German beer stein that had been a wedding gift into a lamp.

hosted regular art openings. Grande dame and client Melba Bennett and her daughter Deedee exhibited their artificial flower and fruit arrangements and holiday table centerpieces. He showed influential ceramist Marguerite Wildenhain's Pond Farm pottery. He also had a rarely seen Bösendorfer piano on display.

Finally, the parched desert received a flood of good design. By 1957 the firm was in full swing with about 30 residential and development projects. They had commissions for redoing the lobby and dining room of the Desert Inn for then-owner Marion Davies, doing the design for Walt and Lillian Disney's second home at Smoke Tree Ranch, and designing a new home for Claudette Colbert on Camino Mirasol. Prolific film producer Eddie Small, who owned a house at 467 Via Lola, hired the firm to add a room; "something that he did every year so that we would have a project and an opportunity to work with him," Hal Broderick quipped. Working on a house for one client and then returning to redecorate it for the next owners would become a common refrain. The Smalls' house was bought by Moss and Kitty Carlisle Hart. "In 1961, after the house was completed, Arthur received a wire from Moss, who'd evidently had some bad relationships with other designers," said Broderick. "Moss said, 'Arthur, if the house is not ready when we arrive, I shall have Kitty and the children parade in front of your shop stark naked with signs saying "Arthur Elrod Is Unfair!"'" Needless to say, the house was ready when they came." The house was later sold to Jeannette Edris Rockefeller (daughter of William Edris and his first wife, Frances Skinner), who moved to Palm Springs after separating from Arkansas governor Winthrop Rockefeller and asked Elrod to redecorate it for her. It then became part of the Sidney Sheldon compound.

Elrod was seemingly everywhere at once. He was constantly on the go, visiting clients and job sites, heading to the East Coast and Europe to see manufacturers and attend trade fairs. The society columns in the *Desert Sun* and *Palm Springs Villager* reported on his every move, as they did with pretty much anyone of note in town. Thanks to jet travel and an airport in Palm Springs, Elrod could fly up to San Francisco to meet with Northern California socialites Mr. and Mrs. H. S. Bonesteel Jr. about their new home in Atherton and be back the next day. He could be in Beverly Hills working on the new home of Glenn E. Wallichs, cofounder of Capitol Records, or Idaho: "Arthur Elrod, local interior decorator, flew to Seattle en route home from Idaho where he furnished and decorated the ranch home of H. C. Berkowitz, distillery executive" (Village Life, *Palm Springs Villager*, September 1955).

In June 1958 he traveled to Boston for the AID convention and then on to Brussels for the World's Fair, also known as Expo 58, on a tour with other decorators. "Everyone agrees that our building at the Fair is beautiful but most report that its contents are very disappointing. On the other hand, eyeing the exhibits objectively and professionally Arthur Elrod found them stimulating. . . . Elrod is likely to be on an Italian kick this winter as he came home most enthusiastic about that country. . . . As though a summer in Europe weren't enough Elrod took off for a couple of weeks in Mexico the minute he got home and should be in high gear this winter" (Around Town, *Desert Sun*, September 16, 1958).

His travels continued the following year: "Arthur Elrod has returned from the jaunt he took to New York to check with eastern manufacturers on new materials and furnishings which he will use in doing the new clubhouse at El Dorado [sic] Country Club (*Desert Sun*, May 27, 1959). "Arthur Elrod is going east this week to Toledo where he will visit the McGowans of Smoke Tree then go on to New York to do some buying for next season. He'll hurry back home though as he is engrossed in two major projects—his own house which he is building out at Smoke Tree and decorating the exciting new Eldorado Club house. He expects to be away just three weeks" (Around Town, *Desert Sun*, June 30, 1959).

Stewart Williams designed the new real estate office for Harold Hicks at 1345 N. Palm Canyon Dr., which opened in November 1956. The Hicks family were pioneers of Palm Springs, and Harold was the top Realtor and insurance broker in town. The one-story structure was sheathed in aluminum with brickwork accents and had refrigerated cooling and forced heat systems. Each office was decorated by Elrod "in the modern vein," wrote the *Desert Sun*, in different colors, from olive green to turquoise to mustard yellow.

Elrod's work extended to nightclubs, as reported in this *Desert Sun* article: "The dining room of Ethel Strebe's new Ethel's Hideaway at Deep Well Hotel has been enlarged and given a glamorous new décor by Arthur Elrod Ltd., decorators" (November 23, 1959). And he also designed offices, as described in this notice about the opening of Harold Hicks's new real estate office at 1345 N. Palm Canyon Drive: "The building, designed by Williams, Williams and Williams, is a one-story structure sheathed in aluminum and accented with artistic brickwork. The lobby and main office, decorated by Arthur Elrod, are in the modern vein, utilizing the dramatic effects of beautiful woods in the walnut paneling and furniture. Each of the broker's offices and insurance departments are decorated in a different color scheme, ranging from olive green to turquoise blue to mustard yellow" (*Desert Sun*, November 14, 1956).

OPPOSITE LEFT: Beginning in 1955, the Sunday *Los Angeles Times Home* magazine frequently published Elrod's projects. The lanai of Marie Green's house in Rancho Santa Fe on the cover of the August 24, 1958, issue. OPPOSITE RIGHT: Elrod contributed articles to *Home* magazine; his first on February 1, 1959, talked about wood grilles (decorative screens) as room dividers. OPPOSITE BELOW: He also served as the editor of the Desert Home Section for *Palm Springs Life*. A model home his firm decorated for the Alexander Construction Co. in Racquet Club Road Estates, with Palmer & Krisel as the architects, was featured on February 12, 1959.

Editorial, Publicity, and Advertising

Along with the *Desert Sun*, *Palm Springs Villager*, and *Palm Springs Life*, the Sunday *Los Angeles Times Home* magazine became an early and regular advocate of Arthur Elrod's work, beginning in 1955. "One day Barbara Lenox swept in in her breathless way and told me, 'Jim, there's this young decorator down in Palm Springs who combines the sand and the dusty gray of the desert with the blue of the sky in his decorating, and I think he's got a lot of promise and we should show him.' That was Arthur Elrod. I don't know how many times we worked with Arthur after that, and it was always a pleasure," recalled James Toland, editor of *Home*, in a 1974 tribute to Elrod. "One reason was that you were not to worry, ever. There were no problems. He was always smiling, always happy about things, and especially about you. Everything you said was important to him. You had the feeling that he was intensely interested in you, above all people."

From 1955 to early 1974, the mass-circulation *Home* magazine featured Elrod's work on a regular basis and frequently on the cover. His debut on January 16, 1955, featured photos of two of his rooms for Bow and Nancy Herbert with white vinyl floors and black floor-to-ceiling shutters; Elrod's own Valmonte Sur home, with a Ruth Asawa mesh sculpture and raised fireplace hearth in the living room; and the new house he had done for Joe and Joyce Pawling.

Barbara Lenox, the contributing design writer for *Home*, would include Elrod in a steady stream of how-to articles on decorator items or "what's new in the decorating world" features. These included introducing a new double vanity for the bathroom, a "trick of the week" that showed a corner table with a rack for magazines, or space-saving ideas like accordion-fold shutter doors that concealed a mini-kitchen in a bachelor apartment. It was a period of exuberant color, and for any article that talked about the latest color combinations, *Home* featured Elrod's rooms front and center, whether he was mixing lime green and acacia yellow with turquoise in a lanai, using red-and-yellow striped wallpaper on ceilings to create the effect of an awning, or combining straw, citron, orange, red, and green leaf in a recreation room.

Elrod had firm ideas about how people should be living and how decorating could improve their lives, and as Toland related, "he felt that *Home* and other shelter magazines were too impersonal, that we should be reflecting how people lived." To get his message across, Elrod wrote a design column for the *Palm Springs Villager*. One of his first articles on February 15, 1958, was about Frank and Melba Bennett's house on Camino Mirasol. He was listed on the masthead as the associate editor of the Desert Home section, and then as the editor of the Desert Living column in *Palm Springs Life* after the two publications merged in 1959. He oversaw the magazine's design coverage, which included articles on other designers and developments that highlighted resort living at its finest.

He also contributed articles to the *Los Angeles Times Home* magazine. His first bylined article on February 1, 1959, talked about the scale of furniture in a room. He discussed the idea of pierced wood grilles, which were prevalent as patterned room dividers. "Personally, I like a free-standing sofa as a refreshing switch from the usual wall placement. Here especially the light, airy quality of the grille lightens the scale of the large sofa," he wrote. His articles stressed proportion, scale, and continuity. "The mark of perfection in decorating must remain—as it does in many lines of art and design—an understatement," he wrote about the *Home* magazine house he designed with architect Richard Dorman.

Elrod was equally savvy at advertising. From the moment he set up shop, the firm placed ads in the *Desert Sun*, *Palm Springs Villager*, and *Palm Springs Life*. The ads appeared on a regular basis, with hand-drawn illustrations of

HOME

Sunday
Los Angeles Times

August 24, 1958

**Desert specimens
for home gardens**
Page 16

**More elegance
for moderns?**
Page 14

George R. Szanik

A Country House at Rancho Santa Fe Page 18

George R. Szanik photographs

This is my best

by Arthur Elrod
American Institute of Decorators

THE IDEA of incorporating wooden grilles in decoration seldom occurs to many homeowners and I think this is because most of us associate them with houses done in the grand manner.

Another reason is that they have been used badly in many instances in modern decoration. Maybe they have an industrial look or they resemble a window display or they're just out of character.

If those are your impressions, you haven't seen grilles used properly.

Grilles, even modern ones, have an Old World character—Spanish, Italian, Moorish. As such they most definitely have a place in our homes—even in our relatively small homes—and I think the one shown here proves the point.

In this large, restyled living room, the grille creates a pleasing entry at one end and screens the rest of the area from the front door. On the entry side a planter box contributes texture and softness to the geometric pattern.

From the living room side the grille solves the problem of placing a large sofa in a room where wall space is broken up by windows, doors and a fireplace. Personally, I like a free-standing sofa as a refreshing switch from the usual wall placement. Here especially the light, airy quality of the grille lightens the scale of the large sofa.

Shelby Willis designed the grille with the idea of creating height in a room by use of tall, vertical panels. The simple wood openings are patterned after a fine antique Italian grille.

---

february 12, 1959

VIEW FROM SNACK BAR into living room reveals a merging of the gaming-dining area. The frames of the gaming chairs are in bright lacquer red and upholstered in white leather.

Resort Living
at its Best

photography by victor culina

SNACK BAR AND KITCHEN are attractively functional. Deluxe kitchen equipment is placed so as to be accessible yet not obtrusive. Range and refrigerator are finished in antique copper. The kitchen window overlooks the pool area and a sliding door (extreme left, out of picture) allows convenient entry to and from the pool area.

(ABOVE) Blending of interior and outdoor hues are in evidence here. The focal point of this living room is the two large sofas which afford comfortable seating for group conversation. The living room window opens onto swimming pool area.

(RIGHT) This view of master bedroom reveals plush yet functional furnishings with sliding glass doors (curtained) which open onto desert landscaping and patio.

PROPER SHADING from the glare of the desert sun is a feature of the entrance way to Racquet Club Estate homes. Architectural design is by the nationally famous firm of Palmer and Krisel. The air conditioned homes cover a 1200 square-foot area, have three bedrooms and two baths and are moderately priced.

The new Racquet Club Road Estates comprise one of the newest residential developments constructed in the Palm Springs area. They are now being occupied. These homes, east of Indian Avenue, near the Racquet Club, boast the most dazzling views Palm Springs can offer.

From the living room window, the desert stretches out below to the east and the San Bernardino Mountains to the north and the awe-inspiring Chino Canyon view of Mt. San Jacinto to the west.

The house was designed by the nationally famous architectural firm of Palmer & Krisel. The three-bedroom, two bath house, covering 1,200 square feet, is designed to overcome the problems of glare and heat. It also makes maximum use of the dramatic view. The house is air conditioned and efficiently insulated for comfortable desert living. Every room

has a view, making an ideal plan for casual Palm Springs living.

The focal point in the living room area is the two large sofas covered in turquoise textured fabric which afford several people comfortable seating for conversation. The large coffee table used in front of the sofas has walnut finished top with practical structural metal base. The view from the living room window opens directly onto the swimming pool area.

The gaming-dining table is of contemporary height and affords both comfortable dining as well as a place for gaming. The frames of the gaming chairs are in bright lacquer red and upholstered in white leather. The lacquer red color is repeated in lamps and accessories throughout the room. The snack bar which separates the living area from the kitchen area may be utilized both as a

separator as well as for serving buffets or breakfast. This cabinet has storage underneath and above the counter height.

The deluxe kitchen equipment makes the kitchen function smoothly. The built-in oven and range and refrigerator are finished in antique copper and make cooking within easy reach of the work counters. The kitchen window also overlooks the pool area and the sliding door from the kitchen provides convenient accessibility to this area.

The master bedroom has full wardrobe storage and ample storage for luggage, etc. The adjoining bath features a sunken tub and an outside door which affords direct access to the pool area. The two additional guest rooms and bath provide additional sleeping for four people.

From the outset, Elrod advertised regularly in the *Desert Sun*. The initial ads were distinctive black-and-white illustrations of the exclusive lines the firm carried—Robsjohn-Gibbings furniture for Widdicomb, Lightolier light fixtures, and Bigelow carpets. He also purchased radio time, a 15-minute program on KCMJ called "Music of Enchantment" that was "presented for your home listening pleasure by the distinguished creator of enchanting interiors, Arthur Elrod Ltd."

Robsjohn-Gibbings furniture designed for Widdicomb—Elrod's preferred source for chairs, sofas, tables, desks, and bedroom sets—that established a striking visual style for the firm. Other ads promoted the carpets and lighting they represented. These early illustrations alternated with photographs from actual projects the firm had completed for clients such as Mr. and Mrs. Harry S. Reid at Diablo Country Club in the San Francisco Bay Area and Sydney and Rachel Charney at Tamarisk Country Club.

As an advertiser, Elrod understood that publications would give him preferential coverage in their home design and design advice columns, or society and gossip pages—Entertainment in the Sun, Around Town with Hildy Crawford, Women of the Desert, and Scene Around. He was very candid in a *Desert Sun* interview about the boost his ads gave business when he first opened. He even bought radio time on local station KCMJ, a 15-minute sponsored program called "Music of Enchantment" that ran Friday through Monday.

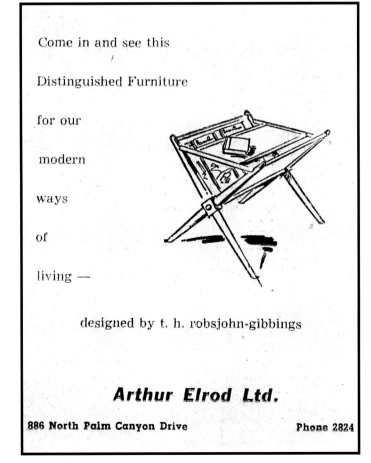
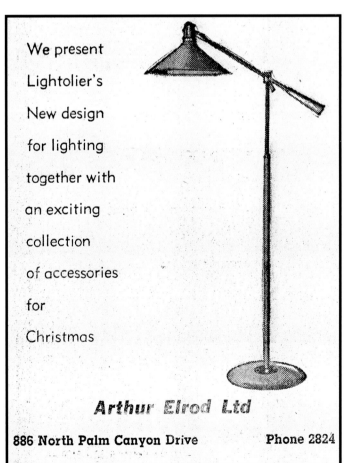

As the desert building boom reached a crescendo in the late 1950s, developers increasingly turned to Arthur Elrod Ltd. to furnish their model homes and touted his name in their ads. Meanwhile, Barbara Wills, who had moved from San Francisco to Palm Springs to help open the Elrod showroom, decided to go out on her own, with songwriter Hoagy Carmichael, who owned a home at Thunderbird Country Club, as the company president and furniture designer.

The Social Scene

Arthur Elrod plunged wholeheartedly into the village's social life. Palm Springs was such a small, tightly knit community that whatever event he attended he was surrounded by people who either were, or would become, clients. He hosted dinner parties at the Racquet Club, sponsored opening nights at the Palm Springs Playhouse, bought a box for the Easter night performance of the Los Angeles Philharmonic, donated decorative accessories and art to charity galas, designed the staging for a musical benefit at the Riviera, volunteered to help hang the curtains at the Desert Hospital, was a judge for Christmas decorations at Jack Meiselman's Palm Lane Estates, donated money toward building a new city animal shelter, and placed ads in every social and charity event program. No deed was too small; no sponsorship request was turned down. In 1956 he was elected one of the directors of the Retail Merchants Division of the Palm Springs Chamber of Commerce and chairman of a fund-raising committee.

He was even asked to comment on Bob Hope's new movie *That Certain Feeling*.

"Arthur Elrod had just dropped into a Swedish Modern chair in his Palm Canyon decorating shop when the *Sun's* reporter popped the question to him as to how he interpreted *That Certain Feeling* in Palm Springs, title of the latest Bob Hope picture to be premiered here May 26," wrote the *Desert Sun* on May 23, 1956. "To me *That Certain Feeling* is the thing that happens to me when I come out of a pool after a swim under the desert stars," he replied. "Swimming at night is a delightfully unique experience and the completely satisfying relaxation that follows is one feeling I'm certain of!"

Model Homes and Housing Developments

The building boom that took hold after World War II became a bonanza by the early '50s and continued pretty much unabated through the mid-'60s. Desert developers were building large single-family tracts, custom homes, shared-amenity condominiums, even mobile home parks. And increasingly, to add value to their developments, they turned to Arthur Elrod Ltd. to furnish the models. It was an ideal situation, especially for larger tracts like Racquet Club Road Estates that were built out in phases. Elrod's firm would decorate the model home in the first subdivision, and when it sold the firm would decorate another one, then do the same in the next subdivision, and so on. What better exposure could be found than to hundreds of potential clients who passed through on model home tours?

Model units for Desert Braemar, the first cooperative garden development in Rancho Mirage, were built in 1955 at the corner of Palm Canyon and Tahquitz Drives in Palm Springs. "Arthur Elrod, interior decorator who handles some of the finest furniture manufactured anywhere, has made a terrific impact on this community with his ideas," wrote Bill Rashall in his Unedited column in the *Desert Sun*. "If you have a yen to get away from the dull browns, greys and sand color of traditional interiors with a startling visual effect visit the model apartments decorated by Elrod for Desert Braemar. That man has actually taken the blue of our beautiful desert sky, the star studded nights and the colorful gardens about us to blend them all into a delightful habitat. He has actually brought the outside inside with his schemes of interior decorating!" (January 5, 1956).

The Elrod name became the gold standard for any developer who wanted to make buyers feel that they were getting their money's worth. "Desert Braemar singled out the interior decorations by Arthur Elrod Ltd., in the model

George de Gennaro

See Page 12

Home Magazine House: A 12-page report

The *Los Angeles Times Home* magazine debuted its first home in Encino in the January 5, 1958 issue. Constructed of "ordinary building materials available to most of us," the house was meant to "reflect Southern California's heritage and forward-thinking approach to modern living." Working with architect Edward Fickett, Elrod was charged with creating family-friendly interiors that mixed antiques with modern furniture. FOLLOWING PAGES: The living areas vibrated with blues and oranges set against William Webb's shimmering handwoven drapes.

For California: Home Magazine House

HERE and on the next eight pages (in addition to two full pages on 32 and 33 as well as short items in between) is a pictorial report on the Times Home Magazine House.

The house was planned, built and decorated with the conviction that the ideal Southern California home ought to reflect Southern California, its heritage, background and, quite conversely but none the less realistically, its forward-thinking approach to modern living.

In this magazine last Nov. 10 we stated that this would be no pointless luxury house, that it would be constructed of ordinary building materials available to most of us, but that the house would use its color, form and furnishings in such a manner as to suggest space, quiet elegance and fine design far transcending the 2200 square feet of livable area.

We believe the house has accomplished its purpose.

It occupies a high, level site in the hills south of Ventura Blvd. in the Royal Highlands development, near Hayvenhurst Ave.

Builders Donald Buhler and Everett Johnston

faithfully executed a plan by Architect Edward H. Fickett, AIA, which called for a residence ideally suited to family traffic (see the floor plan on Page 24). To put meaning into the theme of California living, past and present, Architect Fickett made dramatic use of the adobelike qualities of slump-stone walls, of rough-sawed beams and exposed wooden roof sheathing, of concrete paving tiles, unglazed mosaic tile in the baths and terrace, natural-stained redwood in the entry and, outside, textured stucco. Fickett's most dramatic touch is the unexpected height and scale of room areas which, in his generally open plan, lend to the house a distinction seldom found in one its size.

Upon this unusual background Decorator Arthur Elrod, AID, placed furnishings and accessories that are both modern and antique. It may be said that, because of Elrod's sure knowledge of textures, color and form, the furnishings seem to ignore time, place and labels in favor of interest and comfort. In short, the furnishings truly fit the house, its theme, its occupants.

For further information concerning the materials and furnishings shown in Home Magazine House send a self-addressed, stamped envelope to Readers' Service Bureau, Los Angeles Times, Los Angeles 53.

Space and

George de Gennaro photographs

Family room, *above, with slumpstone half walls dividing it from living area and entry. Floor is pure vinyl manufactured in Alabama, distributed here. Natural teak table and tri-table and chairs are Folke Ohlsson designs. Antique entry light is from Paul Ferrante collection. Sofa is by Martin and Brattrud. Lamp with pleated bookbinding linen is by Ferrante. Below, living area with ornamental Mexican hens created for fireplace wall by Sculptress Betty Davenport Ford; Jane Ellis candles on wall*

For 3 extraordinary photographs of Home Magazine House bedrooms please turn to Pages 32 and 33

color light the living areas

Decorator Arthur Elrod, *right, took full advantage of light, lofty living and dining areas, below. William Webb's hand-woven draperies form background for living area (shown on cover and detailed on Page 2) as well as dining area with its cane-back chairs of natural oak designed by Folke Ohlsson. Stools and dining table are by Teresa McLaughlin, the antique buffet in dining area by Guy Chaddock*

apartments as 'one of the high spots in our selling campaign' " (*Desert Sun*, July 23, 1956). The Royal Air Country Club Apartments at 389 W. Tahquitz Drive were set on seven acres formerly occupied by the historic Desert Inn Mashie Golf Course. Advertised in 1957 as the "first taste of country life in Palm Springs' downtown district," the "country club oasis" was designed by architects Wexler & Harrison with landscaping by Antone Dalu. The 1,460-square-foot model apartment was furnished by Robert Blanks of Arthur Elrod Ltd.

Joe Pawling's Home of Tomorrow at 295 Hermosa Place in Old Las Palmas took the feverish excitement around touring model homes and ratcheted the promotion up a notch. An engineer turned builder, Pawling delighted in adding the latest technology to his homes, and this spec house was his pièce de résistance. Visitors were awed by the retractable glass ceiling in the entry, the living room's custom couch with built-in controls to lower the TV screen from the ceiling, the kitchen with a "glow ceiling" of lights, walk-in closets with automatic lights and refrigerated fur storage, a master bedroom panel that controlled the lights, music, and television, and a timer that controlled the irrigation system. Publicity for the house, which was open to public tours to benefit the World Adoption International Fund (WAIF) chapter in Palm Springs, included flying in actress and WAIF founder Jane Russell as well as society, travel, and design writers. The grand opening was covered in November 1956 by *Desert Sun* society columnist Hildy Crawford in her typical elliptical style:

> For those seeking entertainment . . . or some new way to amuse those weekend houseguests . . . the just-completed Joe Pawling house on Hermosa Place promises to be a mecca for the next ten days . . . Workmen are rushing to get the finishing touches and Arthur Elrod and his staff are installing the furnishings in preparation for tomorrow's opening. There are always last minute upsets, and when a Los Angeles carpet factory burned

> 10 days ago with the drapes and some of the furnishings lost in the flames it pushed Elrod to get replacements but he has and Joe tells me the house will be ready for tomorrow's opening . . . Just arrived is a gorgeous macaw from Africa that will occupy a perch in the living room. The rare and expensive bird (he cost $750) is in the house colors with sapphire and golden plumage, accented by black and white adding one more exotic note to this unusual house. The all-gas kitchen is something every homemaker will find fascinating. On November 20 they are flying down a planeload of Los Angeles press to tour the house. These will include Jim Toland, editor of Home *Magazine;* Caroline Murray of House Beautiful*; and Barbara Hamill of* Sunset.

Elrod's relationship with the *Los Angeles Times Home* magazine grew even closer when the magazine announced that it was building its first actual house as a "forward-thinking approach to modern living." Located in the Royal Highlands development near Hayvenhurst Avenue in Encino, and with Edward Fickett as the architect, the *Home* magazine house was the centerpiece of the January 15, 1958 issue. "The light touch of Arthur Elrod is unmistakable: a rare feeling for the creation of exciting accents against quiet backgrounds, the placing of fine old things with the best that is new." A smaller-scale remodeling project in Beverly Hills done by Elrod for *Home* magazine was featured in the March 22, 1959 issue. In October 1959 he participated in the furnishing of a prefabricated Japanese teahouse that was displayed at the Pan-Pacific Auditorium in Los Angeles during the annual Decorators and Antique Show and again was featured on the cover of *Home.*

Prolific builder Jack Meiselman opened his model home at 264 Debby Drive in Palm Lane Estates, and Elrod furnished it "in contemporary modern, employing new features he displayed at the recent interior decorator's show in Los Angeles" (*Desert Sun*, November 1, 1958). "Mr. and Mrs. Fred Leahy, new Palm Springs residents, have purchased

An authentic Japanese teahouse, prefabricated in Japan, shipped first to San Francisco and then brought to Los Angeles by *Home* magazine, was assembled by a team of experts at the Silver Lake Reservoir before ending its journey at an exhibit at the Pan-Pacific Auditorium. Elrod was in charge of adding lighting and accessories, which included antiques from the Japanese Center in Los Angeles.

Home

Architect, landscape architect and nurseryman consult plans on building site. The tea house, undeveloped, is in background

5 men: a tea house

● Some of the most stimulating designers and craftsmen in Southern California's home development industry helped Home Magazine assemble its tea house and otherwise prepare it for photographic and public exhibition. Architect Kenneth M. Nishimoto, AIA, directed the work by Japanese carpenters who put the jig-saw puzzle together. Landscape architect Curtis Dixon Anderson, AILA, designed the garden and deck and directed installation of dozens of plant specimens and organic material which compose the setting. George Yamaguchi of O. S. Nursery supplied plant materials, including valuable crated specimens, Japanese lanterns and garden accessories, rocks, etc. David Geller of David Geller & Son, landscape contractor, built the susumi-dai, an informal outdoor Japanese deck designed by Anderson. Decorator Arthur Elrod, AID, applied the final touches—paint, antiques, authentic accessories, many of them provided by Marque Richard from the permanent museum collection of the Japanese Center here. The Los Angeles Department of Water and Power joined Home Magazine in supervising the project since the house was erected on department property.

Kenneth M. Nishimoto
Architect

Arthur Elrod
Decorator

Curtis D. Anderson
Landscape Architect

George Yamaguchi
Nurseryman

David Geller
Landscape Contractor

13

In November 1959 the Eldorado Country Club Clubhouse opened its doors. The combination of William F. Cody's superlative architecture with Elrod's interiors produced one of the most sophisticated clubs in the desert, and was the pinnacle of their collaboration. OPPOSITE: An armorial chest and a cluster of antique Spanish candle sconces on a brick wall.

the model home for Jack Meiselman's popular Palm Lane Estates. Meiselman today announced that a new Palm Lane model, also decorated by Elrod, will soon be opened" (*Desert Sun*, December 23, 1958).

In 1959 alone, the Alexander Construction Company was advertising three major developments—Racquet Club Road Estates, Vista Las Palmas Estates, and Golden Vista Estates— and Elrod's firm decorated and furnished the model homes for them all.

Decorator Showhouses and Home Shows

Touring model homes became a major weekend attraction for people looking to buy a house, and so did home shows and decorator showhouses aimed at consumers looking for furnishing and decorating ideas. The two went hand in hand, and Elrod participated in every major decorator showhouse in Los Angeles, usually held at the Pan-Pacific Auditorium, and in Palm Springs at the Pavilion. Decorating a booth or a room meant that he could pull out all the stops while introducing his design concepts to the masses.

"Elrod Exhibit Hailed at Show In Los Angeles—Arthur Elrod has again done a fine job of publicizing Palm Springs," ran the headline in the October 18, 1956 *Desert Sun*. "The room he did for the *Los Angeles Times* in the seventh annual Decorators and Antique Show, which ends Friday night at the Pan-Pacific Auditorium, has attracted much interest. Elrod's room is subtly done in a monochromatic scheme which proves both restful and inspiring while receiving drama from the three color lighting effects which is done from a control panel for mixing the colors using 12 recessed ceiling lights." For the eighth annual show, he created a white and gold bedroom with white and gold silk wallpaper,

a carpet in gold, and an Italian four-poster bed that would be featured on the cover of *House Beautiful*.

Beginning in February 1957, the Palm Springs chapter of the American Association of University Women (AAUW) hosted an annual tour of the town's most interesting houses. That first year, two homes that Elrod had decorated were included. "After ringing an antique brass gong, visitors to bachelor William Boggess' year-round home at 1366 Calle de Maria are greeted in an inner garden by a Japanese statue beside the glass paned door," read the program. "The Ed Robbins' home at 1120 Alejo Road, decorated by Arthur Elrod in the desert shades of green and sand, form a perfect setting for the many beautiful accessories found throughout." In February 1958, the second annual AAUW home tour included the Elrod-decorated home of Frank and Melba Bennett at 1184 Camino Mirasol.

Eldorado Country Club Clubhouse

Elrod would close out the 1950s with a project that would garner national acclaim and heralded his move toward a wholehearted embrace of sophisticated Modernism. When the Eldorado Country Club clubhouse opened its doors in November 1959, it ushered in a new era of golf. The ultra-exclusive club played host to presidents (Eisenhower), celebrities (Bob Hope, Bing Crosby), the world's top golfers (Sam Snead, Jack Nicklaus, Arnold Palmer), and Ryder Cup tournaments, all written up in the press and featured in newsreels.

The clubhouse was like nothing anyone had ever seen before, or would see again. This was William F. Cody's third clubhouse in the desert—he had renovated the one at Thunderbird Country Club, which had been originally created by Gordon B. Kaufmann, and designed the one at

Cody applied his previous experience working on clubhouses at Thunderbird and Tamarisk Country Clubs to propel Eldorado into the future with such innovations as placing the cart concourse under the building so that players could enter without waiting for the starter. Elrod's understated furnishings were perfectly in sync with the architecture.

Tamarisk Country Club. So for Eldorado, Cody, working with architect Stanley Smith of Ernest J. Kump Associates, was able to marshal all his experience and introduce innovations such as placing the cart concourse below the clubhouse so that golfers could drive golf carts directly in and out without having to wait.

Eldorado represented the epitome of golf course sophistication, and the desert was abuzz with anticipation for months. The *Desert Sun* published the first preview on October 29, 1959: "In front of you as you drive toward the building is a large parking area divided by an ever-moving cascade of water over blue and gold tile. It would be utterly impossible to fully describe the atmosphere, beauty and tranquility of this golf course, its buildings and its accompanying facilities. As you enter through the front entrance you walk beside the still-flowing waters, which originates just inside the lobby in a large indoor pool. On this floor of the building are the offices, luxurious dining area, cocktail

lounge, kitchens and private dining room. Going straight through the dining area you find yourself on a porch overlooking the vast expanse of greens and fairways. From inside the concourse on the golf course side a series of pillars allow a view of the Santa Rosa Mountains."

As ever, the loquacious Hildy Crawford wrote about it in her Around Town column in the November 24, 1959, *Desert Sun*:

People who have seen it come away talking in superlatives. It's partly the unbelievable beauty of the setting. The sweeping greens and fairways that are aisles between the palms and the sheltering grandeur of the mountains. It's partly the restrained beauty of the two and a half million-dollar clubhouse with its broad sheltering verandas and its great doors that are castle-size. Inside, it's the freeform room dividers that break up the great expanse of the clubhouse into usable portions, the exciting lamp dusters and the unexpected use of armorial chests which Elrod has combined with ultra-modern, achieving great charm.

Elrod matched the horizontal lines of Cody's architecture with low-slung furniture and a smattering of antiques. He also decorated a handful of homes at Eldorado Country Club Cottages West, including the Presidential Villa for Eisenhower, and he returned in 1965 to gussy up the club's lower-level snack bar,

The 53,000-square-foot clubhouse had the lounge, dining room and bar, golf shop, locker rooms, steam and massage rooms, and barbershop on one level. BELOW LEFT: A corner of the bar. BELOW RIGHT: The ladies locker room. OPPOSITE: A corner of the dining room and wide terrace that overlooked four greens.

which was being enclosed and air-conditioned, "to complement the elegance of the Eldorado structure."

As the 1950s came to a close, he was starting to define the "Elrod look." How to top all that? By being the object of a catty gossip item: "The 'Bel-Air' section in P.S. is still Las Palmas Estates. Talented Decorator Arthur Elrod bows to the whims of the wealthy there—though often in snickering silence. Arthur, Arthur, were you responsible for the Chanel No. 5 wafting through the Moorish mansion of that silver-blond Southerner named Dottie Davis?" (Joan Winchell, *Los Angeles. Times*, January 21, 1958).

You really know you've arrived when you are the subject of

a cartoon. Our Dames, by young local writers/artists George Shaw and Gene Poinc, ran in the society section of the *Desert Sun* and regularly poked fun at "ostentatious Palm Springs matrondom in their natural habitat—a plush bejeweled Palm Springs" (*Desert Sun*, July 30, 1959). For their entry on February 19, 1959, Shaw and Poinc set their sights on Elrod and his wealthy clientele. The cartoon features befeathered and bejeweled guests and their poodles in all their finery at a gala; a wealthy Elrod client is identified by the dollar sign on his hand. The caption: "Oh, how absolutely divine! . . . It must be that new Arthur Elrod décor . . . wall to wall guests . . ."

The 1950s | 75

Oh, how absolutely divine! . . . . It must be that new
Arthur Elrod decor . . . wall to wall guests . . .

THE
1960s

1960s

The 1960s ushered in many transformative changes.

The first happened in 1964 when William C. Raiser joined the firm and a shift, subtle but profound, occurred in its design direction.

Raiser, originally from Jenkintown, Pennsylvania, was a design heavyweight in his own right. He had studied graphic design at New York's Parsons School of Design and was active in its alumni association, serving as president of the National Council of Parsons Alumni Association from 1964 to '66. He worked in New York for industrial designer Raymond Loewy for 30 years as a project director and vice president on commercial interiors, including assisting Loewy with the interiors of Air Force One for John F. Kennedy, the Paris and Orly Hilton Hotels, Northeast Airlines, branch stores for Bloomingdale's and J. L. Hudson, and the Imperial House lobby as well as a line of rugs for Edward Fields and Loewy's DF-2000 series of enameled steel, lacquered wood, and molded plastic furniture.

Raiser was tall, impeccably dressed, and well connected. His New York apartment at 24 W. 55th St. had been shot for *Look* magazine and he had been photographed in his office for a fashion spread. There were many overlaps between his and Elrod's worlds. Stewart Williams had also worked for Loewy in New York early in his career alongside Raiser, and Loewy kept a vacation home in Palm Springs that had been designed by Albert Frey. Loewy would stop by the Elrod studio when he was in town, and he and his wife, Viola, were neighbors and friends with Joe and Nelda Linsk, who owned the Kaufmann House from 1963 to 1971 when it was decorated by Elrod.

Arthur Elrod Ltd. was incorporated as Arthur Elrod Associates on March 21, 1966, and Bill Raiser became a director in 1968. Raiser oversaw the firm's entry into contract work, so they formed a separate division, William Raiser/Arthur

Elrod, to handle the commercial work, which included offices and condominiums. He also took over the design of their rugs and carpets, and shifted the process and weaving over to Edward Fields in New York. Raiser traveled frequently between New York and Palm Springs, so he kept his Manhattan apartment as the firm's East Coast base and he stayed in the guest room at the Elrod House in Southridge when he was in the desert.

There were other transformations as Palm Springs grew and matured into a city:

> *Elrod has seen a vast change in desert living. "Entertaining in the desert is much more formal now," [Elrod] observes. "We are becoming more urbane and cosmopolitan with every passing season. And the décor of our homes reflects these trends. We have lost the charm of the old village, but we have gained elegance." He sees a growing emphasis on the contemporary type of décor here in the Palm Springs area—it's particularly adaptable for modern living and is easy to maintain.*
> —Desert Sun, *February 6, 1962*

Elrod's look started to become more polished, more layered, and much smoother. The *Los Angeles Times Home* magazine described it as "cool sophistication and warm hospitality." No one else captured the relaxed-yet-sophisticated elegance that epitomized Palm Springs living. Elrod welcomed innovations such as the first "full-dimensional" stereo system, which consisted of two full-range speakers integrated with a six-foot-wide curved refactor panel, which he mounted on a grasscloth wallcovering.

Budgets were expanding exponentially. Clients all wanted the Elrod look, and finances were rarely an issue. They were building bigger custom homes on bigger lots designed by a new wave of architects and developers such as James McNaughton, Lawrence Lapham, Ross Patten, and Duke Wild, who ramped up the footprint of homes to more than 5,000

PREVIOUS PAGES: An outtake from Slim Aarons's classic *Poolside Gossip* shoot at the Kaufmann House when it was owned by Joseph and Nelda Linsk. From left: Tennis friend Doug Macy, philanthropist Cliff Lambert, industrial designer Raymond Loewy (standing), Hal Broderick (seated), Viola Loewy (behind Broderick), Nelda Linsk, Steve Chase, Helen Dzo Dzo, Joe Linsk. RIGHT: William C. Raiser, who joined the firm in 1964, and Arthur Elrod. BELOW: An estimate for longtime clients Henry and Nancy Ittleson for their apartment at the Pierre Hotel.

square feet. And they were assembling major art and sculpture collections, mostly early twentieth-century and contemporary works by the likes of Picasso, Rothko, Giacometti, Motherwell, and Noland that required more space to display and more custom furnishings to enhance them. Since Elrod was the one specifying and buying their art and incorporating art and sculpture into all of his projects, it gave him the impetus to commission original works by Andy Nelson, Gene Flores, and Melvin Schuler, among others, for his own homes. Elrod had always championed and encouraged artists and artisans, and he held regular gallery openings at the showroom. This engagement with the art world made it possible for him to approach an artist of the caliber of Robert Motherwell and ask him to create a special diptych for a client's dining room.

WILLIAM RAISER / ARTHUR ELROD

LETTER OF ESTIMATE

RESIDENCE OF MRS. HENRY ITTLESON JR., PIERRE HOTEL, NEW YORK

Outlined below is the revised Letter of Estimate for the furnishing of your residence at the Hotel Pierre in New York City, in accordance with Phase III of our Letter of Agreement dated October 30, 1973.

ENTRY HALL

1. Floor Treatment

   We will supervise the installation of the hardwood parquet flooring in this area. Installation to be billed by William Erbe.   N/C

2. Wall Treatment

   We will design and supervise a general remodeling which will include flush doors and trough lighting. This work to be executed by Herbert Construction Company and invoiced to you directly.

   We will supply and supervise installation of vinyl suede on all walls and ceiling surfaces in this area. Vinyl suede will cost $ 700.00
   Installation will be by Herbert Construction.

3. Door Hardware

   We will supply to Herbert Construction Company the Paul Associates hardware that you have indicated you would like us to use on all of the doors in the entry, gallery and bedroom hall. The hardware will cost approximately

4. Wall Hung Console

   One special lucite wall hung console designed by us and executed by Karl Springer Associates $1,320.00

24 WEST FIFTY-FIFTH STREET, NEW YORK, NEW YORK 10019, TELEPHONE (212) 586-7908
850 NORTH PALM CANYON DRIVE, PALM SPRINGS, CALIFORNIA 92262, TELEPHONE (714) 325-2593

JOSEPH AND NELDA LINSK HOUSE

470 W. Vista Chino, Palm Springs

New York businessman Joseph Linsk had been coming to the Racquet Club in Palm Springs for years to play tennis with friends. In 1962 he brought his new bride, Nelda, who immediately fell in love with the town. The first house the Linsks rented, at 1255 Camino Mirasol, was owned by Claudette Colbert, and had been decorated by Elrod. "We had a July Fourth party and some of those long firecracker sticks burned a hole in the chartreuse shag carpet and then a new puppy chewed the drapes in the family room," recounted Nelda Linsk. "So we had to replace the fabric, which cost a fortune. And we found out later from Arthur that he had a whole warehouse full of it."

The Linsks, who lived in Manhattan and had a country house in Upstate New York, were interested in buying a home in Palm Springs. Their Realtor persuaded them to take a look at Richard Neutra's Kaufmann House at 470 W. Vista Chino. "The minute I saw that sandstone wall I knew it was the house," said Nelda Linsk. The couple bought it for $150,000 in May 1963, but Nelda added, "It was in terrible shape—it had been sitting empty for years. The pool was full of debris, the curtains were hanging off rods." They initially heard about Elrod from friends at the Racquet Club. "We hired Arthur to do the renovations. It was all light, white, and yellow—white

When the Linsks purchased Richard Neutra's Kaufmann House in 1963 they hired Elrod to redo the interiors. ABOVE: Nelda Linsk and her poodle Brandy walking from the living room past the bedroom. OPPOSITE: Nelda at her desk in the bedroom. "My desk was bright yellow enamel, the bedspread was custom woven in beige with matching headboard, and one wall was all floating cabinets," she says

put a tabletop on to seat 8 to 10," according to Nelda. "The floors were terrazzo. We left the planter where the louvers are. The furniture was all McGuire—black bamboo game table and chairs with matching black-and-white tweed cushions, two armchairs and a matching sofa. There was a long entertainment center on the wall facing the guest rooms with a TV and a music system. The sunken bar at the end equipped with an electric ice machine was black-and-white mosaic tile and had five McGuire black bamboo captain's chairs with red leather seats and two black Eames chairs with ottomans. It was a stunning room!"

From the family room, a lawn led down to Joe Linsk's office, which abutted the master bedroom. "Cody designed the office so that visitors could enter it through the family room rather than going through the master bedroom," said Nelda. "He designed three steps into the office through sliding doors. He built a raised bench all the way to the wall from the steps—Arthur had a black-and-white cushion made, great for seating. He left the sandstone exterior wall adjacent to the desk and added bookshelves on the stone wall, and he added a large closet at the bottom of steps coming in from the master bedroom."

carpet, off-white upholstery and drapes, textured fabrics, a mix of antiques and modern furniture. But we had nowhere to sit and have our coffee and read the newspaper in the morning, and Joe needed an office. So Arthur recommended Bill Cody, who added a family room and an office at the back."

Cody took a breezeway and flat concrete pad in the interior courtyard, which was sheltered by aluminum louvers and connected the main house to the guest rooms, and enclosed it. The lanai garden room was, "where we had breakfast, lunch, and dinner, and quite often we would

Dione and Richard Neutra visited the property when it was open for the AAUW Home Tour in 1964, and Neutra reportedly gave the additions his blessing. The house had already been immortalized by Julius Shulman's 1947 photo shoot for Neutra after it had been completed for the Kaufmanns. Thanks to a connection to society photographer Slim Aarons, who also had a house in Upstate New York, Nelda received a call from him in February 1970 asking her to gather some friends for a pool shoot. The resulting *Poolside Gossip* photo with Nelda Linsk and her great friend Helen Dzo Dzo freeze-frames the house at the pinnacle of midcentury chic and has become one of the most recognizable images of Palm Springs.

The Linsks sold the Kaufmann House fully furnished in March 1971 to Eugene and Frances Klein (see page 116) for $350,000. They then moved to 425 Camino Norte, and Elrod gave that house a dynamic entry of mirrored and wood slats that wrapped around the doors and into the living room, brown suede sofas, and McGuire chrome-back chairs. The Linsks bought the lot next door and built a tennis court with a William F. Cody–designed tennis pavilion. Their third house was at 443 Merito Place, on half an acre on the south side of the street with no neighbors. "It had more McGuire furniture—Arthur and I both loved it—with brown upholstery and animal skins," Nelda said. Elrod also decorated their art gallery Galerie du Jonelle, in its second location at 241 E. Tahquitz-McCallum Way. "Arthur was the first person I know of who designed movable panels and wrapped them in padded burlap so that we could put nails in without the holes showing," said Nelda. "We had ever-changing exhibits, so that was important. He was so ingenious." By that point, the Linsks and Elrod had become close friends. Joe could often be found puttering around Elrod's greenhouse at Southridge planting orchids and Nelda became a hostess at many of Elrod's events, including his glamorous New Year's Eve parties.

The Linsks' second house at 425 Camino Norte. OPPOSITE: Nelda Linsk in the dramatic entry hall, photographed for *Town & Country*. "The walls were wrapped in bands of brown lacquered fabric, mirrored glass and wood slats," she said. "The mirror company said it was impossible to do, but Arthur insisted, and when they finished they said never again!" ABOVE: The back terrace shaded by heavy cotton drapes. BELOW: The dining room featured a McGuire glass-topped dining table with a bamboo base, and dining chairs and screen covered in the same patterned red fabric.

The Linsks purchased the lot next door then asked Bill Cody to build a tennis pavilion (above), the scene of many tennis parties. "It was all glass except for one solid wall of cork, and outside was a mosaic tile bar, barbecue, and buffet," said Nelda. LEFT: Tennis pros Charlie Pasarell and Dennis Ralston on the court. OPPOSITE: Nelda Linsk and Arthur Elrod at Galerie du Jonelle, the Linsks' art gallery at 241 E. Tahquitz-McCallum Way.

ARTHUR ELROD HOUSE II

350 Via Lola, Old Las Palmas

Elrod's second home at 350 Via Lola, which he bought in 1957, started out as another modest Spanish adobe. He took the tall profile of his first house on Valmonte Sur and pushed it even further. He raised the ceiling height from 8 to 14 feet and added a stern stuccoed façade at the front with tall entry doors. Massive "statement" front doors were becoming taller, and were usually made of carved teak or walnut and adorned with enormous, ornate Schlage brass doorknobs. Elrod's doors were plain black and sported distinctive, long, turned-brass door pulls made from antique four-poster beds. These opened into an L-shaped inner entry courtyard with a water channel and then to another set of doors with floor-to-ceiling white shutters to the side. It's a purposefully slow reveal that forces visitors to pay attention to every detail.

The entire house is a quietly luxurious testament to the polished Elrod look that now mixed custom furnishings with different textures on every surface, different combinations of materials, and a sophisticated lighting and hi-fi system. "Via Lola is an incredible time capsule, in the best way," said Los Angeles designer Brad Dunning. "That's interior decorating at the highest level. So customized, it's up there with Sunnylands. It was his home and his lab to figure a lot of things out, like combinations of materials and colors. When I started looking for a house in Palm Springs in 1994 it was a Modernist ghost town and I'd see homes with Elrod interiors still intact. Every countertop, every surface, even in condos, was so detailed. You don't see as big a design vocabulary today. Elrod's work was like resort wear—alive and flamboyant, in the best way."

The house was featured in *Palm Springs Life* in August 1962, *Architectural Digest* in Winter 1963, and *Interior Design* in August 1963. Elrod sold Via Lola fully furnished in 1964 to publisher William Hamling and his wife, Frances, who promised they would not touch a thing. Apart from hanging some of their own art, they stayed true to their word. The house, still in the Hamling family, is one of the few existing Elrod interiors that is completely intact.

Elrod's second home, which is still mostly intact, started as another modest structure (above left) that emerged after a complete remodel with an even taller profile. ABOVE: He added a new façade with double doors, brass door pulls from a four-poster bed, and wrought iron grilles. OPPOSITE: An inner entry with a water channel leads toward the second set of doors with similar pulls and pebblestone floors that flow into the entry hall.

At Via Lola, Elrod continued to experiment with texture and color, still mixing antiques with custom pieces. ABOVE: V'Soske wool rug with raised floral pattern in orange, olive, and yellow anchors the 14-foot-high living room; 22-foot-long Prentice sofa and freeform cork coffee table. Glazed brick fireplace wall with cluster of antique Spanish sconces. Wall cabinet finished in pickled walnut houses stereo, TV, and storage. OPPOSITE, CLOCKWISE: Game area with ebony table and olive leather chairs. Entertainment area with zebra skin rug, tufted ottomans in olive silk, Prentice sofa in textured linen against a stone grille. Dining room fireplace wall of glazed wormy chestnut, hand-tufted citron yellow rug by V'Soske on bleached oak parquet. Sunken bar in the entertainment area.

The master suite, which opens to the pool terrace, has walls covered in textured turquoise wallpaper, solid on one side (left) and with a hand-painted mural of white bamboo on the other (below right). Middle Eastern–inspired headboard. Shirred sari silk in turquoise and saffron shade the master bath windows (below left). OPPOSITE: Front pool terrace covered with a stitched canvas lattice on steel columns. Outdoor furniture, terra-cotta stools and accessories all came from Italy. In 1964 Elrod sold the house completely furnished to the Hamling family. "Everything you see here was here. Arthur created it all," said William Hamling. "The guy was a genius."

ARTHUR ELROD ASSOCIATES

850 N. Palm Canyon Drive

Another shift occurred in January 1968, when the firm moved next door into a brand-new studio and offices at 850 N. Palm Canyon Drive. Elrod drew up the plans and gave them to William [Bill] Foster, one of the top builders in town and someone who had worked frequently with Elrod. "I doubt there was an architect involved with the new studio," said Barbara Foster, Bill's widow. "Arthur would have known exactly what he wanted and did it his way."

Mari Anne Pasqualetti, daughter of architect E. Stewart Williams and his wife, Mari, worked for Arthur Elrod Associates from 1968 to 1970. "After graduating from college with a degree in textile design, I returned to Palm Springs and was offered a position with his firm in January 1968," she said. "My father thought it would be a terrific opportunity to involve myself in the world of interior design, and Arthur was gracious enough to find a place for me. Arthur had just moved into a beautiful new building along with his partners William Raiser and Harold Broderick. There were three other designers—one was the newly hired Stephen Chase. I was given the position of being an assistant to Steve.

"Arthur had a strong work ethic. The office opened at 8:00 A.M. and that meant everyone was at their desk, ready to go. When we left for the day, every desk had to be cleared of any debris and look as pristine as his. The environment never encouraged anyone to display personal effects, and no one was ever hired if there was even a hint of this to come.

"You entered the large showroom through a tall steel door, which was fabulous, but during the summer months we could always depend on a scream from a client trying to open the front door when they reached for the knob. We had to put some kind of a covering on it during the days of 120 degrees!

"There was a center corridor with offices on either side that continued to the back area that had additional rooms for accounting, business, etc. There was a back door that looked out on a loading dock and storage area. Within the complex there was also a conference and sample room with additional smaller work areas for designers. Upon entering the central corridor from the showroom, Arthur used the first office, Bill Raiser occupied the second, and Hal Broderick the third. These were all located on the north side of the building. Across from Arthur's office was a reception area with a private secretary for the three principals. Following that space on the south side was a larger room with areas housing four or five desks for other designers and their assistants. The interior finishes of the showroom and offices of Arthur, Bill, and Hal were all constructed with rough-sawn wood on the walls and everything was painted white. The interior of their offices contained beautiful custom-made carpets designed by Bill and made by Edward Fields in New York. The design of the carpets mirrored the design of their desks, which were finished in a high-gloss glaze, very colorful, extremely sophisticated. As you passed these offices down the corridor, the doors and the walls were framed with a frosted glass. The north-facing walls of each were clear glass with an exterior of trees and shrubs, facing the parking area. I remember the showroom floor and corridor being white, perhaps marble. There was wonderful furniture in the showroom, everything for sale but nothing was marked, and our clients really did not view this as a retail space."

In 1968 Arthur Elrod Associates moved into its new studio and offices at 850 N. Palm Canyon Dr., which reflected the firm's increasingly polished, smooth, modern look. OPPOSITE: The tall front door was made of hammered steel. BELOW LEFT: With its high ceilings and rough-sawn wood walls, the all-white studio was frequently the site of photo shoots for the firm's ads. Painting by Andy Nelson. RIGHT: Arthur Elrod, Bill Raiser, and Mari Williams, wife of architect E. Stewart Williams and a trustee of the planned Desert Museum. BELOW RIGHT: The furniture in the studio was a mix of Martin Brattrud kid leather sofa, McGuire chairs, and an Arco lamp.

1960s Design Evolution

By the late 1960s the firm no longer carried Widdicomb or Baker furniture. They used Knoll, McGuire, the Pace Collection, and Wicker Works, but most of their furnishings, fabrics, and rugs were designed in-house and custom-made. Leading furniture designers such as Karl Springer, John Vesey, and Milo Baughman made pieces to the firm's specifications. Their main suppliers were longtime trusted sources in Los Angeles and New York, many of whom are still in business. Sofas came from Martin Brattrud or Prentice. Maria Kipp and Webb Textiles created hand-woven fabrics for upholstery, lampshades, and drapes. Paul Ferrante supplied lamps and ironwork for lighting and railings. Monteverdi-Young did dining tables, chairs, bar stools, sideboards, and consoles. Rugs and carpets came from Edward Fields or Decorative Carpets. Wallpapers, murals, and scenic papers came from Robert Crowder, Van Luit, or C. W. Stockwell. Shutters were made by Anna Mae Devereux. Lacquered finishes were by Richard Wilkinson. Kitchens were designed by St. Charles.

"Arthur's style was elegant, very luxurious, smooth," Mari Ann Pasqualetti said. "I saw his transition from a more traditional look to a more modern one. He had a wealth of experience from his days at W. & J. Sloane, but with the new studio he seemed to be enjoying a new phase. He loved color. I always thought his design aesthetic at this period was influenced by the arrival of Bill Raiser, who was so enthusiastic about modern design. Bill brought a fresh New York eye for the new office and projects." Katherine Hough, former chief curator of the Palm

Hand in hand with open floor plans that let light flood in, interiors of modern homes exploded with color, and this was especially true in the kitchen. Elrod used the latest appliances and technology, and often worked with kitchen designers. OPPOSITE TOP: Built-in barbecue in Lucille Ball and Desi Arnaz's kitchen at Thunderbird Country Club. OPPOSITE BOTTOM: The streamlined kitchen in the 1958 *Home* magazine house in Encino with horizontal freezer-refrigerator. BELOW LEFT: Duane and Marsha Hagadone's lake house kitchen in Coeur d'Alene in vibrant red, yellow, and purple. BOTTOM LEFT: Elrod's meticulous kitchen at Via Lola, with a pass-through with cooktop and waterfall tile. BELOW RIGHT: A glow ceiling of fluorescent lights bathes the laminate cabinetry in the Oklahoma kitchen of Roy and Alta Woods.

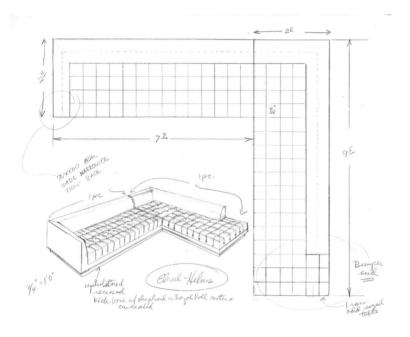

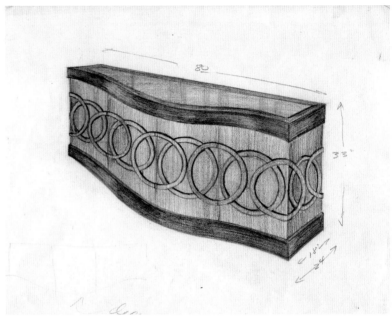

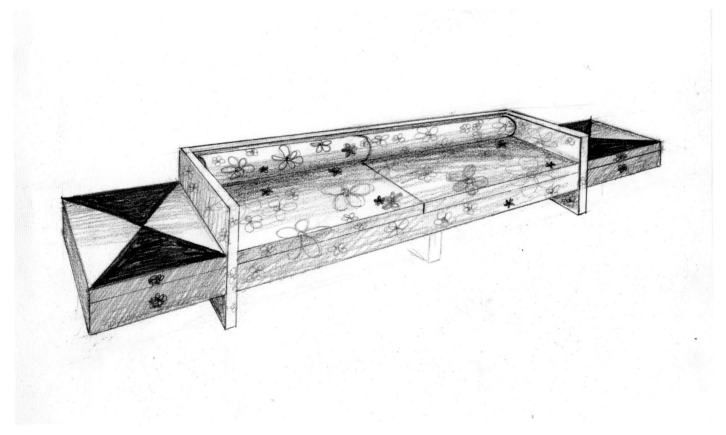

By the late 1960s most of the firm's furnishings were sketched in-house and custom-made by longtime trusted sources in Los Angeles. Elrod's innovations included adding recessed kick bases under sofas, installing concealed stereo speakers in the arms of sofas and in the ends of consoles, placing lighting in sofa bases and underneath consoles, adding automatic lights to closets, raising wall consoles off the floor, and placing control panels next to the bed in the master suite.

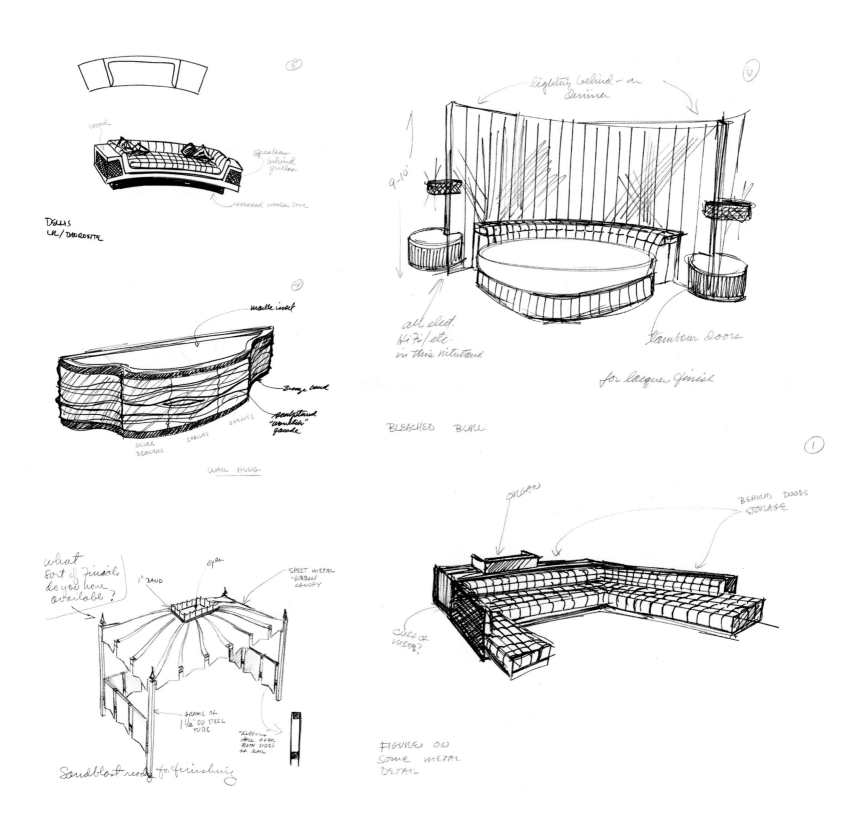

A few homes in Palm Springs still contain furniture specified for Elrod projects. TOP: A floating buffet with speakers at each end, outlets for hot plates on top, and drawers lined with tarnish-resistant cloth. MIDDLE: Karl Springer lizard skin desk. BOTTOM: Backgammon table. OPPOSITE TOP: John Vesey's Maximilian bench. OPPOSITE BOTTOM: Karl Springer dining set with python snakeskin chairs and matching kitchen buffet.

Springs Art Museum, was hired in the early 1970s to turn the firm's furniture sketches into large-scale drawings for cabinetmakers and upholsterers as well as do perspective drawings to show clients. She agreed with Pasqualetti: "Bill Raiser was a big influence. He brought a more pared-down Modernist aesthetic to their interiors and furnishings. The interior detailing became less decorative and more architectural."

"Housewives can match anything" was Elrod's mantra. "We don't match—we blend." Sofas stretched out 20 or 30 feet, the longer and more sinuous the better. Many had speakers built into the arms and lighting installed around the recessed kick base. Every wall unit was raised off the floor and appeared to float against a wall, with no legs to distract from the horizontal plane. Floating buffets for dining rooms were precisely fitted with sliding drawers lined in tarnish-resistant cloth for flatware and silverware, recessed outlets for hot plates, and concealed stereo speakers, and were always underlit. Wall units for dens and bedrooms were engineered to contain television sets, hi-fi systems, and racks for LPs. Beds were equipped with a master console that controlled the lighting, drapes, and music. Televisions were tucked away on hydraulic lifts inside chests. Closets always had automatic lighting. Materials including colored resin, parchment, leather, suede, acrylic, and pierced vinyl, were poked, prodded, and stretched to be smoother, thinner, or more textured. Exotic skins such as crocodile, ostrich, zebra, and tiger—both real and faux—were used for rugs or upholstery in dens and game rooms.

Accessories such as glass, flatware, silverware, vases, paperweights, obelisks, trays, cigarette paraphernalia, candleholders, and boxes were taken on memo at Hudson-Rissman on Melrose Avenue, the leading supplier of accessories to the trade. Lucite bookshelves, cocktail tables, pedestals, stools, ice buckets, mirrors, candlesticks, wastebaskets, tissue boxes, ashtrays, and magazine holders were

ordered from designer Charles Hollis Jones, who provided all the Lucite accessories for Elrod's projects after he set up his own business and had this to say about Elrod:

I met Arthur at Hudson-Rissman in the mid-'60s. You had your screens made at [Robert] Crowder, you got your furniture at Prentice, and you came to Hudson-Rissman for your accessories. I'd started as a truck driver and then became their main designer for about nine years. My first memory is of him coming into the showroom around Christmas-time with baskets of fruit for the people who worked in the factory. He said, "I'd like you to take these to them," because he knew I went to the factory every day. He didn't meet them, he didn't know them, but he was so generous, and that impressed me. He always took the time to talk to us personally. Arthur was very into personal relationships.

"Arthur was an exceptional individual," said Mari Anne Pasqualetti. "He was filled with creative energy and an amazing ability for design, but he also possessed a personal charm unlike others. The one quality that stood out to me was his kindness and generosity to his employees in our office and our workrooms. He would entertain quite frequently at his home and insist that everyone bring their spouses. I departed the firm in 1970 thinking I could follow a Mary Tyler Moore single-girl scenario and find a new, exciting life in San Francisco. Arthur tried to convince me that my future looked brighter if I moved to Dallas, where the world was filled with oilmen! He was gracious enough to send me back to San Francisco, where I landed a great position with another designer."

Elrod, Raiser, Broderick, and the staff spent so much time shuttling back and forth between Palm Springs and Los Angeles to check on suppliers or take client meetings that they rented a small house at 8830 Dorrington Ave. in West Hollywood that functioned as a Los Angeles office and a place to sleep over if need be. Elrod's driver and handyman Lester Cormier was in charge of driving the van from the desert to Los Angeles to pick up completed furniture orders and deliver them.

Home Shows
and Designer Showhouses

As the construction boom petered out in the mid-1960s and the allure of touring model homes faded, home decorating shows and interior design showhouses took over. Crowds now filled convention centers to see the latest in furnishings, fabrics, and appliances. Again Elrod was front and center in Palm Springs and Los Angeles. In January 1961, he created a resort-appropriate lanai room complete with Van Keppel-Green chairs upholstered in all-weather leather and a hammock made of a washable synthetic for the first annual Palm Springs Decorators and Antique Show, which launched with a four-day exhibit at the Palm Springs Playhouse. For the second annual Palm Springs Decorators and Antique Show in February 1962 at the Palm Springs Pavilion, Elrod planned two displays: a dining room with a cork table, lacquered Venetian chairs, and a brass chandelier by his associate Bob Hammerschmidt; and a Persian bedroom with Van Luit scenic wallpaper and sari silk bedspread and bed hangings.

Elrod was on the advisory committee for redecorating the Palm Springs Historical Society's new headquarters, formerly the home of Cornelia White, along with Melba Bennett, president of the society, and Mrs. J. Smeaton Chase. Elrod's home at 350 Via Lola was included in the 1962 AAUW Home Tour. With decorator Dorothy Paul, he designed the California room for DuPont's Pavilion of American Interiors at the 1964 New York World's Fair. The AAUW Home Tour of 1964 featured two of his projects: the homes of Joe and Nelda Linsk and the William F. Cody–designed Waldo and Alice Avery House at 335 W. Vereda Sur with living room furniture upholstered in lime green fabric, tables of rosewood and teak, and bronze and linen-rope outdoor furniture. In October 1965, the second Annual AID Interior Design Show and Furniture Fashions Exposition was held at the Los Angeles Memorial Sports Arena with the theme Good Living in California. With over 400 exhibits, the centerpiece of the show was the AID pavilion, and one of highlights of the pavilion was a $50,000 exhibit by Uniroyal executed by Elrod. According to an article in the *Los Angeles Times*, it included "a furnished living room, bedroom and patio with ceilings and walls covered in Uniroyal Naugahyde by U.S. Rubber." In 1964 he created a morning room exhibit at the newly opened International Design Center at 8899 Beverly Blvd. in West Hollywood, and in 1967 he and Broderick produced a multipurpose family room with piano, bar, soda fountain, game table, and seating in vibrant blue, bitter green, and white, the first in a series of rooms by leading designers sponsored by the *Los Angeles Times Home* magazine at the IDC. For a display at the annual National Hotel & Motel Exposition in New York, covered in the *New York Times*, he showcased a practical motel room that could function as an office with a built-in bed and folding ironing board, a compact shower with fiberglass walls, and weatherproof patio furniture.

OPPOSITE: Elrod still wrote occasional magazine articles and contributed in 1964 to the *Home Magazine Decorating* book with articles on mood and scale. BELOW: In 1967 he and Hal Broderick created a multipurpose room for the new Los Angeles International Design Center at 8899 Beverly Blvd. in West Hollywood. Sponsored by *Home* magazine, the family room was the first in a series of rooms done by leading designers and had a soda fountain, game table, and molded Tulip chairs in a vibrant green and orange setting.

For U.S. Rubber's room display at the annual AID Interior Design Show and Furniture Fashions Exposition at the Los Angeles Memorial Sports Arena in October 1965, Elrod installed a living room, den, patio, and bedroom. Every surface was covered in colorful Naugahyde to demonstrate "maximum wear with minimum care." Main wall had inset panels of Naugahyde, fireplace wall was covered in green vinyl, and sofa upholstered in lemon yellow Naugahyde. Edward Fields rug was of Polycrest, a new deep-pile fiber by U.S. Rubber that was stain resistant. The room extended out to a patio with Brown Jordan furniture, Architectural Pottery planters, and a Patio Royal Vinyl carpet that could be vacuum-cleaned or hosed down.

Model Homes and Developments

Throughout the 1960s, Arthur Elrod Associates continued to be in high demand with desert developers, especially the Alexander Construction Company, which was building out Racquet Club Road Estates, Vista Las Palmas, and Golden Vista Estates. Designed by architect William Krisel of Palmer & Krisel, the single-family homes with air-conditioning and pools in Racquet Club Road Estates and Vista Las Palmas were an immediate hit with middle-class buyers, and have become symbols of how Modernism in Palm Springs was fully embraced en masse. Elrod and Broderick continued with the groundbreaking prefab steel development houses designed by Wexler & Harrison, developed by Calcor Corporation/Rheem Manufacturing, sponsored by U.S. Steel and built by the Alexander Construction Co. Three model homes opened to the public in March 1962. Advertised as "Luxury Look on a Budget," Arthur Elrod Associates furnished one for $3,500.

Elrod participated again in the 1962 *Los Angeles Times Home* magazine House at the Yorba Linda Country Club, this time with Richard Dorman as the architect. It was an

A subdivision of low-cost prefabricated steel homes with three distinct rooflines was planned around Sunnyview Drive by architects Wexler & Harrison, developed by Calcor/ Rheem, sponsored by U.S. Steel, and built by the Alexander Construction Co.

OPPOSITE: Arthur Elrod and Hal Broderick furnished three model homes, which opened to the public in March 1962, in desert tones of mustard, adobe, beige, and moonlight white with tieback drapes. BELOW: The central core (kitchen and bathrooms) of the 1,400-square-foot steel house was fixed, but the configuration of the other rooms was flexible. Steel was the ideal building material for the desert and prefab construction was the solution to cheaper housing, but only seven homes would be completed.

all-electric house, complete with electric oven and heat pump. When it was featured in *Home* magazine, Elrod wrote an accompanying article titled "A Collection of Fine Details." He also personalized a Harlan Lee-Byron Lasky spec house in Encino designed by Dan Saxon Palmer of Palmer & Krisel, which was also featured in *Home* magazine.

More model homes opened at Racquet Club Road Estates: 289 Racquet Club Road in 1961 and 1115 Padua Way in 1962. At the same time, Elrod and Broderick applied for

building permits in 1961 for a house at 2652 Starr Road, which was a small-scale version of Elrod's house on Via Lola and which Broderick called home for a couple of years. Ads in the *Los Angeles Times* in 1963 touted the firm's interiors for two luxury high-rises in Beverly Hills: Reeves Towers at 137 S. Reeves Drive ("the first prestige steel and concrete high-rise residence"), and Spalding Towers at 330 S. Spalding Drive.

Tennis Club president Harry F. Chaddick commissioned William F. Cody to design the new Tennis Club Hotel as well as 39 condominiums down the street. Elrod and Broderick decorated the condo model unit in warm browns and blues, leather furniture, and Webb Textiles' gossamer handwoven drapes.

In 1965 came a model unit in the A. Quincy Jones–designed Country Club Estates at 1989 S. Camino Real; furnished models at Johnny Dawson's Seven Lakes condo development at 4100 Seven Lakes Drive; model condo units in the William F. Cody–designed addition to the Tennis Club; and a furnished Smoke Canyon Estates model at 1453 Plato Circle. Rimcrest, the terraced condo development at Southridge designed by architects Leroy Rose and Harold Carlson (originally called Tropic Hills Estates), was given a complete makeover in 1966 to rejuvenate what the *Desert Sun* described as "Little Hong Kong" into a more luxurious compound:

Rimcrest's face-lifting will include interior decorating in model units by Arthur D. Elrod, AID, of Palm Springs, who also is acting as consultant in other areas of the project. Tentative plans have been made for exterior painting in two shades of soft green to complement the muted colorings of the desert hillside. The new view development Rimcrest, with its spacious and luxurious models at 2110 Southridge Drive by Arthur Elrod and Eva Gabor Interiors, are now available for inspection.
—Advertisement, Desert Sun, *April 7, 1967*

In 1968, the Alexanders (father George and son Bob) had initiated a $10 million home-building program for Palm Springs. " 'I want to focus the attention of the nation upon Palm Springs, with its special type of health-giving halo for people all over the world,' George Alexander stated. Special announcement was also made concerning the formal opening today of a new model home in Mountain View Estates. This home is one of the entrants in the contest of the National Association of Home Builders, which presented an award of National Merit to the Alexander Company earlier this year. The home is furnished by Arthur Elrod, AID, of Palm Springs" (*Desert Sun*, March 15, 1968).

The firm's full-page ads always highlighted their projects. BELOW: A rec room from a spec house at 289 Via Las Palmas that was published in *House Beautiful* in April 1970. OPPOSITE: By the late 1960s the firm had offices in Palm Springs, Los Angeles, and New York, and had established William Raiser/Arthur Elrod to handle its large-scale commercial projects.

Publicity and Editorial

The drumbeat of write-ups in gossip and society columns continued. Joan Winchell of the *Los Angeles Times* wrote, "Arthur Elrod, one of Southern California's most successful interior decorators, proves that you don't have to 'party' to insure success. He attends almost no functions and doesn't answer his phone after business hours" (April 21, 1961).

"A reception for patrons and sponsors of the concert will be held in honor of Artur Rubinstein following the musical event. It will take place in the museum, which once again will be decorated through the generosity of Arthur Elrod" (*Desert Sun*, February 19, 1968).

"An idea that began 10,000 miles away in the village of Nanyuki, Kenya, culminated this week in Joan Winchell, owner of Home Safari and *Los Angeles Times* columnist, and Ray Ryan, owner of the Mt. Kenya Safari Club in that far-off village, announcing a fabulous plan to decorate a home in this country with the ideas and mementoes they've collected while in Africa. Since Miss Winchell has recently built at Bermuda Dunes, it was natural for them to use her new home for this purpose. They consulted Arthur Elrod, who enthusiastically supported their novel idea. Elrod claims this is the first time that African décor has been used so extensively in home decoration" (*Desert Sentinel*, February 18, 1960).

Elrod still wrote the occasional article, including one about the 1962 *Home* magazine house titled "A collection of fine details," and he was part of the book *Los Angeles Times' Home Magazine: Decorating*, published in 1964, contributing basic how-to approaches to decorating problems. The book also included contributions by Los Angeles designers Dorothy Paul, Adele Faulkner, Erna Wine, and Charles Pollock.

Elrod approached everything with great panache. As the firm grew and matured, so did the quality of their ads. Glossy full-page ads were placed in *Palm Springs Life* and *Architectural Digest*. He built trust in his clients, and they in turn would entrust him with multiple projects and know

that when they stepped inside their brand-new home, it would be absolutely perfect—from the lighting, art, and furnishings down to their preferred brand of cigarettes in the cigarette box and their favorite candy in glass dishes. "I guess it's like finding a favorite hair stylist or doctor," said one client for whom Elrod was working on his sixth house. "You never let him go!"

ARTHUR ELROD ASSOCIATES
850 N. Palm Canyon   Palm Springs, Calif.   714 325-2593
Residential and Commercial Design

ARTHUR ELROD, A.I.D.
WILLIAM RAISER, A.I.D.
HAROLD BRODERICK, A.I.D.
BOB HAMMERSCHMIDT, A.I.D.
TRACY THORNTON, A.I.D.
STEPHEN CHASE

ARTHUR ELROD ASSOCIATES Residential Desig
WILLIAM RAISER/ARTHUR ELROD Commercial Desig

850 N. Palm Canyon   Palm Springs, Calif.   714 325-2593
8830 Dorrington   Los Angeles, Calif.   213 272-5796
24 West 55th Street   New York City   212 586-7908

ARTHUR ELROD, A.I.D.
WILLIAM RAISER, A.I.D.
HAROLD BRODERICK, A.I.D.
TRACY THORNTON, A.I.D.
STEPHEN CHASE
DOUGLAS T. BARNARD, A.I.D., A

EUGENE V. AND FRANCES KLEIN HOUSE

410 Trousdale Place, Beverly Hills

"If there is one feature associated with the work of Arthur Elrod, it's a sort of bachelor pad swank that shows up even in his houses for happily married men and their wives," said Steven M. Price, author of *Trousdale Estates: Midcentury to Modern in Beverly Hills.* "The zenith of this ethos would be expressed via Englishman Ken Adam's set designs for the James Bond films of the 1960s. 'Bond villain lair' is more compliment than warning in this world. In 1961, however, the notion didn't exist yet (*Dr. No*, the first Bond film, debuted in 1962), which makes Elrod's collaboration with architect William R. Stephenson at the behest of client Eugene V. Klein (sportsman, conglomerate chief, and bon vivant), in the anything-goes Trousdale Estates section of Beverly Hills all the more prescient.

"The sky's-the-limit décor of the Kleins' crab-shaped house featured all those highlights we'd come to expect later: curved walls seamlessly clad in walnut; deep-pile wool shag carpet, stepping down into one of the first conversation pits on record, directing eyes out over the pool to the city-lights view and predating the luxury sports stadium skybox Klein would champion later; a sunken, circular wet bar; the use of conference room–like seating around the dining table and midcentury sculptural shelving in the family room; grass-cloth walls on the curving art gallery—better to hide the nail marks when a picture was removed or replaced; custom parchment-covered tables, together with inviting, beckoning sofas and club chairs sheathed in his signature voluptuous velvets, and of course woven silk draperies at the 14-foot-high sliding doors. This was all Elrod, though it was designed to convey the power of the man who might welcome you in, make you rich, or dash your dreams. Gene Klein Interpreted, if you will, in the same way Arthur would later direct John Lautner to 'give me what you think I should have on this lot.' Not 'give me the house I want' . . . but giving the design force the power to think Bigger, be Better, to venture Beyond."

OPPOSITE TOP: The travertine façade of the 6,000-square-foot circular house by architect William R. Stephenson in Trousdale Estates, Beverly Hills. OPPOSITE BOTTOM: Elrod and Frances Klein in the living room's lower sunken level, which was created to take in the views. ABOVE: At 6 feet 6 inches, Gene Klein towered over Elrod. The Kleins' art collection included works by Moore, Giacometti, Picasso, and Léger. RIGHT: At the other end of the 38-foot-long living room was the travertine-topped semicircular bar.

OPPOSITE: Walnut doors opened to the dining room, with marble floors, ebony dining chairs upholstered in sapphire blue and black, and a buffet with a bronze silver-leaf finish. TOP LEFT: The master bedroom in cobalt blue and green had a curved travertine fireplace wall and a blue lacquered floating console. BOTTOM LEFT: Frances Klein in her bathroom. BELOW: Semicircular colonnades shaded the outdoor terraces.

LAURENA HEPLE, DIAMOND HEAD APARTMENTS

2969 Kalakaua Ave., Honolulu, Hawaii

With a portfolio of homes in Pebble Beach, Palm Springs, and Los Angeles, all decorated by Elrod, the peripatetic Laurena Heple and her second husband, Walter Bratney, added a pied-à-terre in Honolulu. She was a dynamo, the maker of the Sky Scooter for the air, and the Desert Rat dune buggy and the Pacer for the trail; he was one of the biggest manufacturers of remote-controlled gates. Their ocean-view apartment in the Vladimir Ossipoff–designed Diamond Head Apartments that overlook Kapiolani Park and Diamond Head was featured in the *Los Angeles Times Home* magazine on March 1, 1964.

OPPOSITE TOP: Arthur Elrod and longtime client Laurena Heple at Honolulu airport. OPPOSITE BOTTOM: For Heple's pied-à-terre at the Diamond Head Apartments, Elrod mixed Oriental objects with pieces from her Pebble Beach house. By the entry to the living area was a carved chest and a wall unit hand-lacquered in Peking yellow which held a TV, stereo, and writing desk. BELOW: The *mauka* (mountain) lanai was a small space made larger by low-lying furniture and varying textures—cork flooring, cane sofa, animal prints, leather drum table.

OPPOSITE: The living room, which overlooked Kapiolani Park, was in shades of yellow, saffron, and bronze. BELOW LEFT: Game area with card table and leopard print chairs. BELOW RIGHT: Master bedroom had walls papered in gold shadow print, repurposed gold-leaf screen from Pebble Beach, bedspread of bronze-gold silk, and emerald green for the bench and chair upholstery and accessories.

ALTA AND ROY G. WOODS HOUSE

7428 N. Country Club Dr., Oklahoma City, Oklahoma

Alta Woods was introduced to Elrod's work when she saw his own home on Via Lola, which was part of the sixth annual AAUW Home Tour of 1962. She and her husband, Roy, a founder of petroleum, transportation, and manufacturing companies, hired Elrod to design their main residence on the seventh tee at the Oklahoma City Golf & Country Club.

Completed in 1966 by architect and Oklahoma City native Howard Lapham, the 9,000-square-foot house had a

rectangular travertine façade that stretched over 225 feet. Elrod's elegant interiors melded with the contemporary structure, starting with 12-foot-tall entry doors handcarved in India that sported 7-foot-long brass door pulls. At the home's core was a skylit central atrium with a reflecting pool that was defined by a series of carved wood grilles. The main rooms had 12-foot-tall windows that overlooked wide terraces framed by massive columns that led to the pool and paddle tennis court.

OPPOSITE: Architect Howard Lapham's contemporary design for the Woods House in Oklahoma featured a 225-foot travertine façade. OPPOSITE BELOW: Striking 12-foot front doors hand-carved in India faced the skylit central atrium that was defined by wood grilles, a portrait of Alta Woods, and marble slabs over a water channel. Dining room with Diego Rivera painting. BELOW: Focal point of the club room was a sculpted bronze wall sheet by King Zimmerman. All pieces of furniture and objects were individually spotlighted. V'Soske carpet went from off-white in the center to saffron yellow at the edges, coordinated with Maria Kipp upholstery.

OPPOSITE: The pool cabana overlooked the seventh tee of the Oklahoma City Golf and Country Club. Bar surround is multicolored tile. RIGHT: The club room's game area with glove leather chairs and octagonal game table. BELOW: Alta Woods's bedroom with a custom Persian themed wallpaper by Robert Crowder, four-poster bed with finials that matched the mural's minarets, and bed posts, nightstands, and cabinetry lacquered in mother-of-pearl by Richard Wilkinson.

ABOVE: With a ceiling wallpapered to look like a tent, the playroom for their grandchildren featured a crafts table and wall unit for toys as well as such modern accessories as a color TV and record player. Plastic pedestal chairs were equipped with a "memory swivel" so that seats returned to their original position. BELOW: Alta Woods's marble bathroom. RIGHT: Guest room with a variation of the Robert Crowder scenic wallpaper.

ALTA AND ROY G. WOODS HOUSE

40995 Thunderbird Road, Thunderbird Heights, Rancho Mirage

Built in 1960 for Hyatt Robert von Dehn, one of the owners of the first Hyatt hotels, the Woods' 10,000-square-foot vacation home in Thunderbird Heights was even larger than their Oklahoma residence. Elrod was given carte blanche and four months to complete the renovation. A portico of tall travertine columns opened to a newly added skylit entry atrium, similar in concept to their Oklahoma home, with a reflecting pool that flowed under steps of travertine marble and plexiglass. The palette purposely veered from subtle earth tones used in private rooms to vibrant colors for public entertaining spaces. Outside was a bar, a pool terrace paved in black terrazzo that led down to the pool, with a sunken marble dance floor and raised terrace for an orchestra, and a pathway that led to the guest house, tennis court, and tennis pavilion.

ABOVE: **For their vacation home in Rancho Mirage, Alta and Roy Woods chose another Howard Lapham–designed home, also with a grand motorcourt entrance and façade of tall travertine columns with tall narrow windows. Built for hotelier Hyatt von Dehn, the house was enlarged to 10,000 square feet.**
RIGHT: **Elrod's interiors alternated a subdued palette for the living room and family areas with vivid colors for the entertainment areas, such as the bar.**

ABOVE: Dining room had two lacquered and chrome dining tables for seating up to 16, six-foot-long chandelier of Venetian glass cylinders, and pecky cypress paneling. OPPOSITE: The game room and bar zinged from jet-black lacquered cabinets to zebra skin fabric on the black walnut bar to brilliant red Pierre Paulin Ribbon chairs and red Andy Nelson artwork. BELOW: Master bedroom's bed and nightstands were finished in mother-of-pearl. Another first for the firm was designing a motorized TV set that rose from a chest in the sitting area.

LEFT AND BELOW: Alta Woods's bathroom suite and closet. "She would have her staff drive out from Oklahoma with an air-conditioned trailer with her clothes in it so that they wouldn't be wrinkled when they got here," said Hal Broderick. "And then when she wore the outfit, it would go back into a box and be shipped back to Oklahoma. She only wore things once." BOTTOM: Roy Woods's carpeted dressing area had cork walls, travertine counters, and dark wood cabinetry; the mirrored vanity with theatrical bulbs was for shaving. Beyond was the bath and shower, which opened to a sunning garden. The home gym, with weights, machines, and built-in TV, was the first that the firm installed.

Since the desert vacation lifestyle revolved around the outdoors, Elrod created assorted entertainment areas on different levels, themed by color in case anyone got lost. LEFT: Adjacent to the tennis court was the red bar. BELOW: The lower-level poolside terrace, which was paved in black terrazzo, was furnished with Warren Platner's steel rod pieces for Knoll, covered in Elrod's signature sunny yellow. Wall sculpture by Robert Seyle. Nearby was a sunken marble dance floor and platform for a band.

THE
1970s

Exuberant color defined the firm's 1970s projects. PREVIOUS PAGES: Louise and Lionel Steinberg's Buff & Hensman House in Old Las Palmas (see p. 144). OPPOSITE: Bill Raiser designed all the firm's rugs, which were made by Edward Fields in New York. The studio at 850 N. Palm Canyon Drive was frequently the backdrop for the firm's ads. Here the aubergine-painted wall had a custom Edward Fields wall hanging above a sectional white leather sofa.

Design and Color Revolution

As the 1960s segued into the '70s, the color palette used by Arthur Elrod Associates, which now consisted of Elrod, Raiser, Broderick, Bob Hammerschmidt, Tracy Thornton, Steve Chase, and Douglas Barnard, exploded with crimson reds, emerald greens, peacock blues, zinnia yellows, burnished bronzes, and jet blacks. It was a saturated color palette always used exuberantly, skillfully, and with great restraint. "Color is not easy to do," emphasized Los Angeles designer Brad Dunning. "Other decorators of the period were doing similar work, but no one did it better than Elrod—bold colors that were so ballsy, but he pulled it off. I constantly admire how he could mix things and it never looked vulgar, cheap, or garish. He could do those patterns and bright colors on a par with the best Color Field painters of the time like Kenneth Noland, Ellsworth Kelly, or Frank Stella, but he was doing it in 3-D."

"I walked into the very beautiful studio of Arthur Elrod's in Palm Springs in 1973 immediately overwhelmed by the 15-foot high walls finished in a deep aubergine color," recalled Marybeth Norton Waterman, who began her design career there as "a very naïve 19-year-old, hair down to the waist, with a miniskirt to almost meet it." She continued, "Arthur's curved, underlit, tightly upholstered sofa dominated the space and anchored the room's volume. A large abstract painting offered the saturated colors that Arthur was in love with. First impressions are lasting, and it was clear Arthur was fearless with color."

"I was thinking about his use of color," said Brad Dunning. "Those interiors of his and his associates do look somewhat aggressive, foreign, and certainly flamboyant and playful through today's narrow eyes. Then I was thinking that at that time people were wearing clothes like his interiors and driving up to the houses in cars of those colors. We certainly proceed monochromatically through life now—cars, clothes, interiors. So if people look at those

period color-saturated kaleidoscopic Elrod interiors now, they certainly can honestly say they look 'dated'—they are. But don't we appreciate period cars and movies, furniture and clothes with much admiration? That might be how we consider those interiors. They are of a time, but they are the best of that time."

The firm was continuously innovating and experimenting with different fabrication techniques, always eager to give their clients something unique, always intent on staying on the cutting edge of technology. "Arthur had an amazing curiosity about commercial materials and how they might interface into his custom pieces of furniture," Marybeth Waterman said. "He was pouring surfboard resin over fabric and creating countertops with a 'nod to mod.'" This new process was mentioned in the August 2, 1970, *Los Angeles Times Home* magazine: "Fabric can be laminated onto any furniture, walls, doors, even ceilings, with a heavy coating of polyester resin. Designers have only begun to explore its potential. Arthur Elrod, AID, has used it over an exciting design as bar tops in this Palm Springs home. He also suggests it for a coffee table to match a sofa, perhaps a chair to match an end table." He stayed current with European design trends by pilgrimaging to Milan for the latest in accessories and furniture and returned with new ideas and contacts to keep his edge.

Any traces of anything traditional or French Provincial had been erased. "We are living now," Elrod told *Architectural Digest* in 1972. "Homes should reflect the materials and craftsmanship of today rather than the past."

"His design approach was miles ahead of its time," said Marybeth Waterman. "He was the master of midcentury design, and his circle of friends reinforced this, considering that Raymond Loewy, John Lautner, and A. Quincy Jones would stop by the studio for a chat." Katherine Hough added, "Arthur was an innovator. He was the first to do recessed indirect lighting, sofas with recessed kick bases, buffets floating on wall panels. He was very interested in meshing lighting with interior architecture. He didn't just plop furniture down; he integrated the lighting with the furniture and rugs."

"Arthur and Bill Raiser would team on larger commercial projects throughout the country, and together created interiors at the corporate level that had never been experienced," Marybeth Waterman said. "The Johnson Publishing Company headquarters in Chicago was a terrific example of how Arthur would bring a luxurious, residential quality infused with color to an environment that demanded a different vibe. At the time, Chicago's surrounding colony of high-rise towers was flush with Steelcase files, fluorescent lighting, and steno chairs. Projects like this caught the attention of commercial developers throughout the country and opened up another extension of Arthur's focus and talent. He went beyond the clichéd thought that decorators were window dressers, and he contributed to a more respectful profile by engaging early with architects and builders. This complete focus would force a cohesive project and promote a healthy relationship with the team members."

Elrod was of medium height, around 5 feet 7 inches, but he commandeered the room. "My first meeting with Arthur was very fearful," said Marybeth Waterman. "His expression was penetrating. His personal style in dress was so refined, very Savile Row." His salesmanship skills were legendary—he was a master of convincing people with his presentations. "Arthur Elrod exuded a charm with his clients that was of 'star' quality, and they worshiped him," she added. "The clientele would jet in from across the country to meet briefly with him. I say briefly, as he would have drafted renderings, floor plans, and architectural-quality drawings on the table, explain the one-off design of a piece of furniture or cabinet, and then bid them farewell."

THE CUSTOM WOOL WALLHANGING IS BY

EDWARD FIELDS

Even after working with the same clients on multiple homes over the course of two decades, Elrod never addressed them by their first names and rarely socialized with them. "Arthur was very correct and always called his clients Mr. and Mrs., at least until they paid him," noted Paige Rense-Noland, editor emeritus of *Architectural Digest.* "He was the one who persuaded them to look at their second or third house on a par with their primary residence. He made clients want to spend money on their weekend houses."

"As an employee, he demanded the best of service, the best of appearance, and the best of social grace," Marybeth Waterman said. "I always remember him saying, 'Very important! We are in a service industry, we enter our clients' home through the service door, we address them by "Mr. and Mrs.," and never assume that they are your best friends.'"

"The office was equally formal—the men dressed in perfectly tailored suits and everyone was addressed by their last names. "Arthur wasn't spontaneous. He was very controlled, very disciplined," said Katherine Hough. "But he was sincere and respectful."

The firm had perfected the art of the installation and the reveal. "Before clients arrived to see the house for the first time after it was completed, Arthur insisted that the front porch or deck or driveway be hosed off so that when they arrived there was no sign of us being there," said Hal Broderick. "Arthur was a total perfectionist," said Mari Anne Pasqualetti. "He expected the very best from all of us. When we presented clients with their new interiors, the level was astonishing. We had installed all their clothing in their closets, gourmet items in the refrigerator, fire in the fireplace, lighting to give a particular mood. We had all slaved to make every surface glisten, nothing out of place. It was a remarkable tutorial for me, and my husband has never forgiven me for my entertaining aesthetic to this day."

That high-gloss sheen of Arthur Elrod Associates matched the aesthetic that the newly hired editor of *Architectural Digest* was seeking for the magazine. Paige Rense-Noland credits Elrod along with Angelo Donghia, Michael Taylor, Jay Spectre, Anthony Hail, and Mario Buatta with helping her turn *AD* into an international powerhouse in the 1970s. "My history, the history of the magazine, and the history of Arthur Elrod are just so closely entwined that they really can't be separated," she noted during a keynote speech she gave at a symposium on Arthur Elrod at the Palm Springs Art Museum on February 12, 2005. Rense-Noland, now editor emeritus, was hired as an associate editor in 1970 and became editor in chief shortly thereafter. "This was not a job anyone was terribly anxious to have," she recalled. "It

paid very little and I can safely say the magazine was not the most respected magazine in the world. It was well known in certain circles, and it was respected in certain circles, but the problem was that because there was no photography budget, everything had already been in at least one or two other magazines. So I decided that we had to show everything first or it couldn't be in the magazine. Enter Arthur Elrod and Hal Broderick.

"Arthur and Hal were much better known than the magazine. The feeling was that they were Palm Springs—if you had a house or wanted a house in Palm Springs, there just wasn't anyone else. They were the go-to people. And so I got to know them and they became friends. But their professional contribution was much more important to me because when I started my editorial philosophy was 'something on every page.' There was no inventory, so I was very candid. I said, 'I want to show wonderful work, I want to

Interior Design
ARTHUR ELROD ASSOCIATES
Palm Springs

show your work, and I need material.' And they pitched in and they came through. And it was such an important turning point for the magazine because they were so respected in the world of interior design nationally. Everyone knew their work, and so if they gave their work first to this magazine based on the West Coast, which was not a plus in the eyes of Easterners, then it must be all right. And that's why I will be eternally grateful to Arthur and Hal."

The firm's principals worked independently on their own projects and each built up their own clientele, but they came together on larger-scale jobs. In May 1970, Elrod, Bill Raiser, Hal Broderick, Bob Hammerschmidt, and Tracy Thornton hosted Design Horizon '70, sponsored for Southern California members of the AID and American Institute of Architects at the Tennis Club in Palm Springs. The firm designed the exhibits, the keynote speaker was architect John Lautner, a film on Ray and Charles Eames was shown, and that evening

Elrod hosted cocktails, dinner, and dancing in a tent at his home. Elrod and Lautner worked together on a vignette of rooms titled Gentleman's Retreat for the annual AID Interior Design Show and Furniture Fashions Exposition held at the Hollywood Palladium. In January 1971, the Martin Anthony Sinatra Medical Education Center at Desert Hospital opened. Dedicated to the memory of Frank Sinatra's late father, the center was designed by Donald A. Wexler Associates with interiors by Arthur Elrod Associates. Groundbreaking on the new Palm Springs Desert Museum took place in January 1973; Elrod and Raiser consulted with architect E. Stewart Williams on the interior finishes, detailing, and upholstery in the museum and the Annenberg Theater. Raiser and Steve Chase collaborated on the model condo unit for the Cricket Club complex in Miami. Three model condo units at Twin Springs designed by Donald Wexler were decorated by the firm, with a furnishings budget of $80,000.

The last job that Elrod installed was a house for Weight Watchers cofounder Jean Nidetch on Benmore Terrace in Brentwood. "It was done for Christmas 1973," said Hal Broderick. "We had a full staff of 10 and we had the run of the house and use of the kitchen. We were amazed that the freezer was full of ice cream and candy bars and we didn't understand this in a Weight Watchers house, but she had a 14-year-old son, so that explained it."

By the 1970s, budgets for the firm's major projects were running into the six and sometimes seven figures. Elrod was working with John Lautner on homes for Bob and Dolores Hope on Southridge, and the Marbrisa House for Jeronimo Arango in Acapulco. The firm was also starting a million-dollar renovation of the former Kaiser Estate on Oahu for the Goldman brothers and planning a home on the Costa Smeralda in Sardinia for the Aga Khan.

Arthur Elrod Associates was stepping onto the international stage.

JOSEPH AND WIKI DENNIS HOUSE

41915 Tonopah, Thunderbird Heights, Rancho Mirage

What better way for Joseph and Wiki Dennis to take advantage of the panoramic views of five country clubs from their lot high up in Thunderbird Heights than a round house? "They came into the shop one day and said they wanted a round house," said Hal Broderick. "Everything in the house was round—the master bedroom had a king-size round bed, the Jacuzzi in the bathroom was round." Builder Ross Patten of Patten-Wild created a 90-foot-diameter main house paired with a smaller-scale matching game pavilion surrounded by water. Instead of structural exterior walls, vertical steel beams radiated out from the center of the house and the floor-to-ceiling windows were curved. Elrod associate designer Bob Hammerschmidt took on the interiors, using white and cobalt blue in the living areas and hot pink and crystal in the master bedroom. The circular lavender and chartreuse kitchen at the hub of the house had a large clerestory dome overhead to provide sunlight.

ABOVE: The Dennis' round main house ringed by round pools. BELOW: Ross Patten of Patten-Wild designed the 90-foot-diameter structure with steel beams radiating out from the central core, which contained the kitchen. OPPOSITE: Lit only by a ceiling dome and clerestories, the kitchen gleamed in chartreuse and lavender on the cabinets, sunburst vinyl floor, wallpaper, and paint.

OPPOSITE: Elrod associate Bob Hammerschmidt used white as the unifying color with Wiki Dennis's favorite cobalt blue as the accent, starting with front doors flanked by mosaic glass panels. The round fireplace had a mirrored wall that reflected the living room and sunken bar. ABOVE: Georgia MacLean painting created specifically for the dining room. BELOW: The "gin room," as the Dennises affectionately called the game room, was a 24-foot-diameter replica of the main house reachable by a walkway over the moat-like pool and furnished with aqua blue game tables and yellow chairs.

LOUISE AND LIONEL STEINBERG HOUSE

300 Merito Place, Old Las Palmas

Louise and Lionel Steinberg already had an Elrod-designed house in Palm Springs at 797 Via Vadera, but around 1972 they bought the house at 300 Merito Place that actor Laurence Harvey had commissioned from Buff & Hensman. "The house wasn't completed for Harvey—he was going through a divorce," said their son, songwriter Billy Steinberg. "My parents moved in and finished the interiors, but they divorced after a year. I remember Arthur Elrod well from the many meetings at the house. When he walked in the door you felt his creative presence. He was impressive, passionate. He and my mother had a great rapport, one of mutual respect.

"My mother was entirely involved in the interiors—she was a very sophisticated, very social woman with fine taste in design and food and very passionate about art. She wasn't someone who could be convinced to like something. She would never say 'Get me a dining table' without being involved in its selection.

"The front was very austere, but when you walked inside, the house took your breath away. To the left was the pool with granite rocks. To the right you walked under a covered walkway past glass windows alongside the house and through sliding glass doors into the living room. She and my father had put together a pre-Columbian art collection, and the display case—an enormous custom-designed case with sliding glass shelves—was stunning." With a sunken tennis court, a massage room with sauna, and various entertaining areas, the house was described in *Town & Country* as a "private country club."

A house commissioned from Buff & Hensman by actor Laurence Harvey, but not occupied by him, was completed by Louise and Lionel Steinberg. BELOW: The entrance was reached by walking under the overhang alongside the pool to the front door. OPPOSITE: The covered walkway, which continued left, bridged the pool and the tennis court, and housed a bar and outdoor lounge, sauna, and massage room.

ABOVE: Elrod replaced a bar by the front door with glass-shelf cabinets that held the Steinbergs' collection of pre-Columbian artifacts. RIGHT: The sunken living room and multicolored tufted rug were remnants from Laurence Harvey's ownership. "My mother wouldn't have elected to have that sunken area," said her son, Billy Steinberg. "It wasn't very practical and no one went in there." OPPOSITE TOP: Custom dining table of walnut with chrome inserts and base, Brno dining chairs. OPPOSITE BOTTOM: Elrod designed most of the furniture for the library, including the chrome V-legged desk.

LEFT: Lionel Steinberg's master bath was composed of stone walls and travertine marble floor. BELOW: A guest bedroom in red and blue. Painting of Palm Canyon Drive by Estelle Rogers Weiss, a family friend and wife of noted psychoanalyst Joseph Weiss. OPPOSITE: The existing tufted rug determined the colors of the master bedroom. Figural composition over the bed is a trapunto quilt by Gary Mauro. Art in the house ranged from large abstracts to drawings by Chagall, Picasso, Renoir, Rouault, and Walt Kuhn.

JOHN AND EUNICE JOHNSON APARTMENT

The Carlyle, 1040 N. Lake Shore Dr., Chicago

After publishers John and Eunice Johnson purchased two units on the 24th floor of the Carlyle and merged them into one apartment, Eunice flew to Palm Springs to interview Elrod and Raiser. "She knew exactly what questions to ask. You could tell she had studied interior design. She hired us almost immediately, and so began a marvelous two year relationship," said Bill Raiser in *Interior Design* (October 1972). "We informed the designers that we would like the apartment to complement our two complexions in tones of browns and beige. We felt this type of setting would be comfortable and flattering," said Eunice Johnson.

"Elrod was a great artist and a great human being," wrote John Johnson in his autobiography *Succeeding Against the Odds: The Inspiring Autobiography of One of America's Wealthiest Entrepreneurs*. "We hit it off from the beginning, and he created a fabulous apartment. He told us up front that he wouldn't take the job unless we agreed to leave all of our old furniture in the old house. Two weeks before the job was completed, he made us promise not to visit the apartment until he was satisfied with the arrangements. The big night came and he called and said, 'I want to invite you to dinner in your new apartment.' When the door opened, I couldn't believe my eyes. It was like something out of *Dynasty* or Hollywood. Elrod took us on a tour and we sat down to dinner prepared by a caterer. It was almost like visiting a rich relative, except it was our own place.

"After Arthur Elrod finished our Lake Shore Drive home, he asked us to spend a weekend with him in Palm Springs," Johnson wrote. "We fell in love with the place and started spending our Christmas holidays there." The Johnsons purchased a home on Southridge north of Elrod's, which had been owned by Chicago businessman Ralph Stolkin, but this was one Johnson project that Elrod would not decorate.

John and Eunice Johnson spent years planning their ideal home in their heads while purchasing artworks by Picasso, Marino Marini, and Chagall, which all found a place in their Chicago apartment. OPPOSITE: The entire palette revolved around variations on brown and beige. Foyer with a ceiling of wood circles on plaster, herringbone parquet walnut floor, swirled Edward Fields rug, smoked glass table, and, in the living room, an Elrod favorite—a Ruth Asawa looped wire sculpture. ABOVE AND RIGHT: Living room walls were made from textured barn siding strips; zebrawood coffee table with burnished brass edges repeats the wall striping.

ABOVE AND LEFT: **Every surface was given a different treatment, all in hushed earth tones. The dining chairs were Karl Springer suede and dyed snakeskin over steel.** OPPOSITE: **The breakfast room had a patterned wallpaper and shelves that held Picasso ceramics. Since the Johnsons entertained frequently, the kitchen had a family side and a catering kitchen with four refrigerator-freezers, two stoves, three dishwashers, and a charcoal barbecue pit.**

JOHNSON PUBLISHING COMPANY HEADQUARTERS

820 S. Michigan Ave., Chicago

John and Eunice Johnson, publishers of *Ebony* and *Jet*, were intent on providing their staff with a Chicago headquarters as groundbreaking as their magazines. The architect they chose was John Moutoussamy, an African American Modernist architect. The designers they chose were Arthur Elrod and Bill Raiser, whose William Raiser/Arthur Elrod division was created specifically to handle all commercial designs and who were finishing work on the Johnsons' apartment. "Even before Elrod completed the apartment he said he wanted to do the new office building. He said he'd never done one and that he would give me a reduction in price if I would give him a free hand," wrote John Johnson in *Succeeding Against the Odds*.

"The Johnson Publishing Co. building was a daring social statement, a monument to the ingenuity and determination of Johnson and the people his publications represented," wrote Maurice Berger in the *New York Times*. As the corporate headquarters, the building also was a showcase for black culture, including the architecture, vibrant colors, contemporary furnishings, and art. "The horizontals, the glass, the marble, the fabrics, the warm colors. All these

elements integrated into one grand design express the essential meaning of our firm—openness: openness to truth, openness to light, openness to all the currents swirling in all the Black communities of this land," wrote John Johnson.

Raiser and Elrod elevated the design of the 11-story building to the level of a private residence, imbuing every floor and every office with rich textures and bold Pop Art and psychedelic patterns that embodied an "Afrocentric Modernism." Each corporate group had a different design scheme, and no pattern was repeated. The elevator interiors were refurbished quarterly to reflect the colors and motifs of the seasons. Bronze surfaces and smoked glass prevailed, along with thick carpeting, leathers, suedes, lacquers, and handwoven wall fabrics. "We spent more time on custom design and detailing than any other job," Raiser told *Interior Design*. "We shipped by 40-foot trailers and flew many craftsmen from Los Angeles to Chicago." Art and sculptures came from Nigeria, Liberia, Mali, the Ivory Coast, and Upper Volta, and were displayed alongside works by contemporary African American artists.

LEFT: **The cafeteria with bold geometrics in yellow, orange, purple, and white embodied the company's "Afrocentric Modernism."** OPPOSITE TOP: **The Trophy room housed civic and professional awards as well as letters from well-known personalities.** OPPOSITE BOTTOM: **The two-story lobby of the Johnson Publishing Company, which had its grand opening in May 1972, glowed with richly textured red upholstery and 18-foot walls of travertine marble, bronze, and Mozambique wood. The entire building was a paean to African American architecture and art. Each floor had a different design scheme and no pattern was repeated.**

The 11th floor was John Johnson's private domain, with an executive office, apartment, and dining room. The office was a rich, tactile cocoon of suede, Hermès leather and burlwood paneling, credenza, and desk; the desk had controls for the lighting, music, drapes, and doors. Johnson's apartment had a sauna in the bathroom and an exercise room with a barber chair. OPPOSITE LEFT: With its laminated fabric in a psychedelic swirl and a central food preparation center, the 10th floor all-electric test kitchen was where recipes for *Ebony* magazine were tried out.

SIGMUND E. EDELSTONE APARTMENT

Drake Towers, 179 Lake Shore Dr., Apt. 23E, Chicago

One of the firm's most exacting clients was Chicago industrialist, philanthropist, and art collector Sigmund E. Edelstone. His 5,000-square-foot apartment in Drake Towers was completely gutted and reworked by architect Ernest A. Grunsfeld III to provide a pristine background for his exceptional collection of abstract art. "This apartment has changed the entire life of its owner," Elrod told *Architectural Digest*, which featured the condo in the May/June 1972 issue.

"While Arthur and I were working on the interior, Mr. Edelstone was acquiring paintings and sculpture," said Bill Raiser. "He brought color photographs of the art to us and then we considered how the paintings would look in the apartment. Neither color nor fabrics were finalized until Mr. Edelstone had bought all the art for that particular room." The three-year project was a meeting of perfectionists who shared the same philosophy. "Mr. Edelstone was already in tune with our thinking, and his understanding of the importance of perfecting each detail of the interior design made our collaboration a pleasure," said Elrod.

Edelstone had shopped in Paris for Porthault linens and Baccarat stemware, all custom made for him. Upon his return, he noticed how bland the elevator lobby on his floor was, and he asked the designers to redo it with suede-covered walls, marble floors, a Viennese crystal chandelier, and custom-designed panels for the elevator door portals.

Every piece of furniture was custom made by Prentice in Los Angeles and shipped in two 40-foot trucks. Workers from Prentice were flown to Chicago to assemble the large sofa inside the apartment. "After the installation we asked Sig how he liked it," said Broderick. "He replied, 'The carpet is a quarter inch off square.' So all the furniture came off the rug, it was shifted, the furniture put back and he was satisfied. After his first night in bed we got a terrible call from him. 'Something's wrong!' 'What's wrong, Sig?' 'There's a gray vein in the white marble surround in my window. I want it out!' And so it was changed."

OPPOSITE TOP: Purity and abstract art reigned in Sigmund Edelstone's Chicago condo. "I don't like clutter. I'm a purist," the 72-year-old bachelor told *Architectural Digest.* Even the elevator lobby received attention, with marble floor and suede walls. OPPOSITE BOTTOM: Picasso's *Woman with Pipe* on white linen walls in white living room. All furniture and rugs were designed by Bill Raiser and installed on-site. ABOVE: Painting by Rothko, sculptures by David Smith and Barbara Hepworth, tub chairs, and steel pedestal table topped with Carpathian elm. RIGHT: Game room and study. FAR RIGHT: Master bedroom with Picasso's *Red Nude,* which dictated the color scheme. Bed was lit from underneath and had a pop-up leather headboard.

SIGMUND E. EDELSTONE CONDO

130 W. Racquet Club Road, Palm Springs

Sig Edelstone had been a winter visitor to Palm Springs for 25 years before acquiring two units at the Racquet Club condominium complex that Arthur Elrod Associates turned into one. As in Chicago, Edelstone wanted a simple, contemporary backdrop for his art collection as well as a flexible space for entertaining. From the distinctive stainless steel–faced gates and front door to the tall Alexander Liberman sculpture poolside, the 1,800-square-foot condo was a meticulously planned and efficient machine.

Each wall was scaled and built to house Edelstone's art, and all the lighting was fitted precisely to illuminate it. The dining area had two tables with round swivel chairs that were lit individually. The floating wood and chrome buffet in the dining area contained silverware drawers lined with tarnish-resistant cloth, a stainless steel top for hot dishes, recessed outlets for hot plates, Lumiline indirect underlighting, and concealed stereo speakers at each end. A built-in desk system in the master bedroom contained a television set, storage for LPs, a fax machine, filing drawers, and a wastebasket. The bedside console controlled the lights, music, and television. Steel control panels were integrated as vertical strips with no switches. All the plumbing fittings were customized.

Edelstone was as much a perfectionist with his vacation home as he was with his Chicago residence. "We had the travertine floors laid end to end, and when Sig saw them there were two black lines that ran through the floor," said Hal Broderick. "He said, 'Oh, I don't like those.' So we had the marble man cut them out and he took the edges of the tile that were defective, put them in a case, flew to Idaho, went to the mill where they came from, matched them exactly, and had the new tiles shipped back and replaced."

ABOVE AND BELOW: **Steel-faced front gates and front doors of Sig Edelstone's condo in Palm Springs.** OPPOSITE: **The den, with a view into the master bedroom, had a painting by Wojcieck Fangor and gazelle sculpture in the stereo/TV cabinet. "Mr. Edelstone has a great eye for scale," said Elrod. "He can tell if something is off $^1/_{16}$ of an inch."**

OPPOSITE: The master bed console panel controlled lights, stereo, and the bed, which was centered in the room. The desk unit held a TV ("constantly going with the stock market all the time," said Hal Broderick), storage for record albums, fax machine, file drawers, and a wastebasket. BELOW: Edelstone wanted a flexible layout for entertaining. The living room had a double-sided sofa, one side facing the fireplace, and bar with sliding pocket doors. "I, personally, am taking on your job and will be devoting my time to this project and will be totally responsible for all aspects," wrote Elrod on July 17, 1973.

ABOVE: Dining area had two tables and swivel tub chairs. Floating buffet contained speakers at each end, steel top for serving, and drawers lined with tarnish-resistant fabric. Charles Hinman painting. BELOW LEFT: All the control panels were integrated vertical stainless steel strips. BELOW RIGHT: The firm presented their best clients with silver Tiffany cigar boxes, this one engraved underneath "Sig, Bill, Arthur." OPPOSITE: Light filters through vertical blinds into the living room. Outside by the pool rose a tall red sculpture by Alexander Liberman.

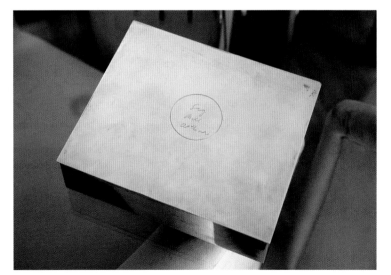

DUANE AND MARSHA HAGADONE COMPOUND

Stanley Hill, Coeur d'Alene, Idaho

On the shores of Lake Coeur d'Alene in northern Idaho arose a small compound for newspaper publisher Duane Hagadone and his family that consisted of their residence at Stanley Hill, the corporate headquarters built over the lake, and a summer log cabin called the Lake House. Constructed by local architect R. G. Nelson and designed by Elrod (Lake House), Raiser (headquarters), and Broderick (the main residence), the compound was a complex undertaking. "We've never done anything like it before," Elrod told *Architectural Digest*.

The Stanley Hill residence in Casco Bay was a contemporary home on 15 acres with stables, enclosed tennis court, swimming pool, and a pond that became an ice-skating rink in winter. The home's basement featured a regulation bowling alley, billiard table, and dance floor.

The 11,000-square-foot headquarters was constructed on three levels at the end of a wood pier that had been a railroad depot for unloading timber from lake boats.

The summer Lake House, fronting a 600-foot beach, was built in 1932 of hand-crafted logs with high vaulted ceilings and was a short speedboat ride from the headquarters. Elrod injected it with sunny, bright shots of yellow, orange, and green based on the colors of a Pacific Northwest totem pole.

BELOW LEFT: The back of Duane and Marsha Hagadone's residence in Coeur d'Alene, with cabana, pool, hot tub, and tennis court. Around the corner was a pond/ice skating rink. BELOW RIGHT: The pool cabana had a bar and kitchen behind louvered shutters. OPPOSITE: The living room, designed by Hal Broderick in monochromatic beige and caramel, centered around a sunken conversation pit and fireplace with a suspended chimney to ensure that nothing interrupted the views. Dining area was on one side (above), raised bar at the other (below). All of the lighting was recessed; even the sofas were lit from underneath.

Duane Hagadone's corporate headquarters for his newspaper chain sat at the end of a wood pier that had been a railroad depot for offloading timber from lake boats. Rebuilt by architect R. G. Nelson, the three-level, 11,000-square-foot structure had pier-level parking, entrance and reception/conference areas on the second floor, and corporate offices on the third floor. OPPOSITE TOP: The entrance ramp to the offices. OPPOSITE BOTTOM: Doors into the reception area. ABOVE: Massive wood posts and low horizontal planks, skylights, and a planted central atrium defined the third floor offices, which were designed by Bill Raiser.

ABOVE: The third component of the Hagadone compound was the Lake House on Casco Bay, accessible only by boat. Built in 1932, the summer cabin made of 1,800 hand-peeled cedar logs was a gloomy affair before Elrod got his hands on it. RIGHT: He took the colors of a Pacific Northwest totem pole as the guide for his primary palette of red, green, and yellow. Carpet was made of bands of woven goat hair. BELOW: The front porch with Wicker Works furnishings. OPPOSITE: Small casement windows were replaced with larger ones, which improved the lake and mountain views in the dining room where two tables allowed for versatile seating.

Three small bedrooms were turned into one large master suite. ABOVE: The bath and dressing room with vaulted ceiling. OPPOSITE: The bed was raised on a platform to take advantage of the views. In contrast to their more formal main residence, the Hagadones wanted a "fun playhouse feel" for the Lake House, and Elrod turned the primary greens, yellows, and reds into geometric patterns on the bedspread and wall covering that repeat the pattern of the logs.

E. HADLEY AND MARION STUART HOUSE

Diamond Dragon Ranch, Bellevue, Idaho

E. Hadley Stuart Jr. was the heir to the Carnation Company. His wife, Marion, was actively involved as a board member and supporter of leading mineral, gem, fossil, and natural history museums (the Los Angeles County Museum of Natural History and the Page Museum at the La Brea Tar Pits in Los Angeles, and the Smithsonian Institution), and was a hands-on participant in fieldwork and excavations.

Their Diamond Dragon Ranch in Bellevue, Idaho, was their main residence and showcase for their numerous collections of rare coins, pre-Columbian artifacts, gems, minerals, and specimen rocks from Marion Stuart's archaeological digs. The house, completed in 1972, was gray shingle with tall granite pillars. The jaw-dropping living room measured 50 by 72 feet with 30-foot-tall ceilings and a pair of 18-foot-tall custom armoires to display Marion Stuart's collection of glass. A write-up of their housewarming party, which Elrod attended, in the *Los Angeles Times* described the house as "decorated in shades of gray with pillows in crushed-raspberries-and-cream pink, lime green, and deeper green pillows, ceiling-to-floor windows that reveal a view of cattle grazing lands, aspen trees, the Wood River, mountains as a backdrop."

Set within the 1,600-acre Diamond Dragon Ranch in Wood River Valley, Idaho, stood Dragonwood, the gray shingle 13,000-square-foot contemporary house of E. Hadley and Marion Stuart. ABOVE: Massive stone pillars at the back of the house interspersed with statues of Pan shaded the terrace with furnishings in green silk.
OPPOSITE: Doors from the entry hall opened to the dazzling living room, which was a controlled symphony in raspberry and lime sherbets and silks.

Measuring 50 by 72 feet with 30-foot-tall ceilings, the living area was part entertainment/dining space and part museum for the Stuarts' collections of pre-Columbian artifacts, specimen rocks, and items from Marion Stuart's archaeological digs. A pair of 18-foot armoires displayed her collection of glass. Rare coins were arranged under glass at the bar counter. Gray was the predominant color for the Edward Fields rug, sofas, and large ottoman covered in chinchilla.

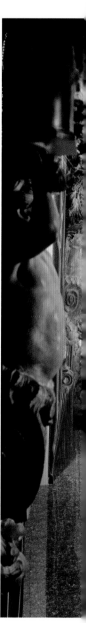

OPPOSITE: A mezzanine floor above the living room had white furniture lacquered by Richard Wilkinson with Fortuny fabric, hand-carved wood lamps, and ribbed chenille carpet. LEFT: The entry hall's highly polished gray marble floor, gray wall covering, and raspberry upholstery. ABOVE: The bedroom of the Stuarts' daughter Nan had a four-poster bed with carved finials of musical monkeys.

THE ELROD HOUSE

2175 Southridge Drive, Palm Springs

By the mid-1960s, Elrod had tired of the endless cycle of buying, remodeling, and selling his own houses. He wanted something more personal, more distinctive, more permanent. On December 6, 1965, he paid $27,500 for Lot 2 of .64 acres on Southridge Drive, the narrow rocky ridge that defines the southwestern end of Palm Springs.

In 1960/61 Southridge Development Co. partners Richard Rahn, Alan Petty, and William Anable incorporated Southridge Estates as a 22-parcel tract that offered a guard-gated enclave with panoramic views and underground utilities designed to appeal to high-profile people who wanted privacy and security. To attract buyers they commissioned a handful of spec houses by Ross Patten and Albert ("Duke") Wild, and William F. Cody. In 1962, Swiss industrialist Max Stoffel bought one of Patten & Wild's spec homes, Chicago industrialist Stanley Goldberg purchased the 1963 Cody spec home that was then personalized by Elrod, and Edwin (Buddy) Morris, a longtime client of Elrod's, had moved into a Hugh Kaptur–designed spec home commissioned by Thomas Griffing that Elrod furnished. In 1965, when the second phase of Southridge opened, Bob Hope bought nine lots at the top.

Why did Elrod approach John Lautner instead of a Palm Springs architect? He was seeking something

Arthur Elrod's house on Southridge Drive, completed in 1968, was a triumphant collaboration with architect John Lautner. Floating under a circular concrete dome, the living room furniture matched the structure's motion with a round Edward Fields rug and Martin Brattrud arced sofa and backless bench, with Palm Springs spread below and the San Jacinto Mountains as a backdrop.

unique, something that pushed the boundaries, something that hadn't been seen in the desert before. An introduction came through his friend Marco Wolff Jr., a Los Angeles interior designer who had just worked with Lautner on his own house at 8530 Hedges Place in the Hollywood Hills. "Lautner designed a house in 1961 for Marco Wolff, and Wolff had connected the architect with a couple of other clients," says architect and author Frank Escher. "Regardless, Lautner would have known of Elrod and Elrod would have known of Lautner." A memo from Elrod to Lautner on August 11, 1966, confirms this: "Talked with Marco and he said he had talked with you and that complete house plans were ready . . . "

Arthur Elrod, being an interior designer, knew much more than most people about houses, but he wanted something more. When he came to see me, he had seen some of my work. He said, "Give me what you think I should have on that property." The typical client would be much more fussy and finicky and not understanding the whole idea, but he was looking for architecture.
—*John Lautner, quoted in* The Spirit in Architecture: John Lautner, *a film by Bette Jane Cohen, 1991*

The two-year project became a collaboration of equals who respected each other's work. For Lautner the result was one of the most significant commissions in his career, one of the few houses he created where the interiors were treated on a par with the architecture, and where the furnishings complemented and enhanced the structure. "Mr. Lautner liked Arthur Elrod's designs," says Helena Arahuete, chief architect in Lautner's office and now principal of Lautner Associates–Helena Arahuete Architect. "He was one of two designers whose work he admired. The other was Michael Taylor, with whom he worked on the Beyer House in Malibu."

"Up till the early '60s most of Lautner's projects were small, modest houses," says Frank Escher. "In the mid-'60s there was a shift. Lautner started working on much larger projects—Silvertop, Chemosphere—and on using concrete as an architectural material and not just as a structural element. So the Elrod house was a very important, pivotal project. Lautner did it for relatively little money because he hoped that by doing the house for a leading designer it would lead to other big projects, and it did. It led directly to the Hope House. And it led to Arango. They had seen the Elrod House published and their lawyer called Lautner to see if he'd be interested in a project in Acapulco. Elrod was supposed to do the interiors of the Arango House—there are still some pieces of furniture in the house that he designed. For Lautner, Elrod was the ideal client, enlightened enough to let the architect do what he did best."

"Southridge is one of Lautner's major works from the second part of his career," says architect and author Alan Hess. "It is so distinctive in how it sits on its site and in Lautner's use of concrete as sheltering roof—he used a lot of big roofs to shelter space. It's an incredible chapter in how you design with concrete."

Design and Planning, 1966–68

The first correspondence between them is a letter dated May 10, 1966, from Elrod addressed to "Mr. Lautner." It included a deposit of $1,000 and requested a contract, which was signed on May 11. Lautner was to be paid a professional fee of $4,000 for the plans, plus construction costs. "November Building Exceeds $1 Million. Another shot in the construction arm was the permit issued for a $125,000 dwelling to Arthur Elrod at 2175 Southridge. The Elrod home was the largest item of three dwellings for which permits were issued in November" (*Desert Sun*, December 1, 1966).

Lautner started work on drawings and schematics and by August 1966 had a complete set of plans to show Elrod. The rocky outcroppings were the site's strongest element and defined the resulting design. "I had this whole lot excavated another eight feet to expose the rock outcrops so that we could make a design that was integrated into the desert," said Lautner. "The first design and model I made he loved,

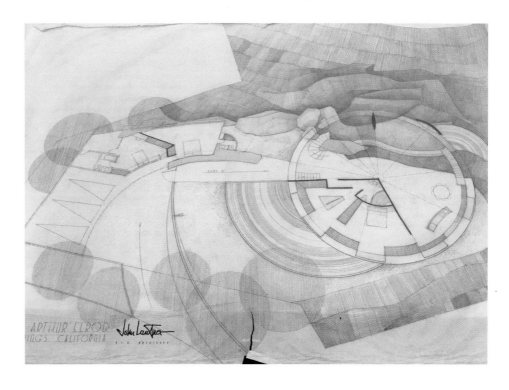

ARTHUR ELROD
...GS CALIFORNIA   John Lautner

and we went ahead and did it." The building permit was initially denied because of assorted code violations, but those were all corrected and construction began in early 1967. Lautner brought on board builder Wally Niewiadomski, who had mastered the art of pouring concrete under Frank Lloyd Wright. After a progress visit to the site in June 1967, Elrod wrote to Lautner enumerating some minor changes they had discussed—"different entranceway to living room, a cantilevered deck, a new plan for the guest bedroom"—but ended the letter, "Needless to say, I am thrilled with the progress of the project."

Architectural Details

Stripped down to its essentials, the house consists of one giant circle and one long rectangle. The circle encompasses all the public spaces—living and dining area, kitchen, guest room, powder room, and terrace. The rectangle is the private side—a 60-foot-long space delineated by furniture groupings into a study/office and bedroom and then dressing room and bathroom suite. A series of circles announces the arrival at the house—curved motorcourt wall, carport, sculpture garden, entry walkway—and ends with the semi-circular pool at the ridge's edge.

The conical canopy sheltering the living area is a 30-foot-tall and 60-foot-diameter poured concrete marvel divided into nine ribbed concrete wedges segmented by clerestories. "By doing it this way it's almost like a desert flower and these clerestories go around so you get different sunlight as the sun moves around. It fits right into the desert," said Lautner in *The Spirit in Architecture*. In his preliminary drawings, Lautner had marked the exact angles where the sun set. Seven of the nine clerestories were capped with triangular, copper roof panels that tilt upward to filter in light by degrees. The

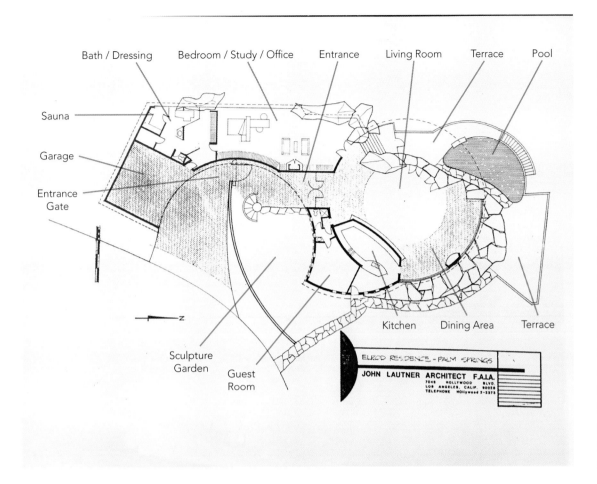

Bath / Dressing   Bedroom / Study / Office   Entrance   Living Room   Terrace   Pool

Sauna

Garage

Entrance Gate

Sculpture Garden   Guest Room

Kitchen   Dining Area   Terrace

ELROD RESIDENCE - PALM SPRINGS

JOHN LAUTNER ARCHITECT F.A.I.A.
7046   HOLLYWOOD   BLVD.
LOS ANGELES, CALIF. 90028
TELEPHONE HOllywood 2-2378

OPPOSITE LEFT: **The cross-section shows three views from a seated or standing position—down toward Palm Springs, across to the mountains, and up to the sky. "The clerestories catch the different light of the morning sun and solve the problem of west sun and view,"** Lautner noted. OPPOSITE RIGHT: **Elrod during a site visit in 1967.** LEFT: **The floor plan of the two-bedroom, 5,700-square-foot house reveals the sequence of circles, from the front privacy wall out to the pool.**

two that jutted out over the terrace and pool were open to views of Mt. San Jacinto and the sky.

Concrete, glass, copper, wood, and slate were the main materials used in the five-room, 5,700-square-foot residence. In keeping with his philosophy of organic architecture, Lautner integrated the site's massive boulders and rock outcroppings into the structure. Walls were given a ribbed texture by pouring concrete into wood board forms. The copper-sheathed entry gate was designed on a pivot; the 16-foot-tall glass front doors were frameless. Black slate was laid in a herringbone pattern all in one direction from the pathway that travels from the carport to the entry, down into the living/dining area through to the kitchen. Floor-to-ceiling glass panes zigzagged around the edge of the living room to cut down the glare and were mitered at the seams so that no frames would disturb the views. A curved fireplace delineated the space between the dining area and a corner seating area. The elliptical-shaped kitchen behind the curved living room wall had St. Charles steel cabinets—the wall cabinets faced in rich courbaril wood and the base cabinets in gray plastic laminate. Past the bedroom suite, a set of stairs illuminated by lights covered with copper plates

led down between rock outcroppings to the outdoor terrace and pool. The half-moon-shaped pool perched at the ridge edge was filled to the brim and spilled down over the concrete wall, a vanishing-edge technique that Lautner had first experimented with at Silvertop. The final construction cost, according to *Architectural Design*, was $300,000.

Design Details

While Elrod placed an emphasis on custom furniture and extravagant finishes for his clients, he switched things around for his own home. Many furnishings were custom made, and everything followed the curved motif. The 24-foot-long arced sofa with chrome supports that faced the view and a matching 16-foot backless bench were designed by Elrod, fabricated by Martin Brattrud, and upholstered in a burnt orange Jack Lenor Larsen seamless fabric stretched taut. In the center of the living room was a round 25-foot Edward Fields rug designed by Bill Raiser in neutral colors with a raised pattern of circles that repeated the architectural refrain. Glass cocktail tables with cylinders made of large Pyrex chemical beakers held Charles Hollis Jones's

OPPOSITE: The driveway, with the curved motorcourt and carport (top). The structure's ribbed texture was achieved by pouring concrete into form boards. Black slate, laid in a herringbone pattern all in one direction, ran from the driveway down past the sculpture garden toward the glass front doors (right). The bedroom and carport roof was planted with yellow zinnias (left). ABOVE: Lautner designed the frameless copper gate on a pivot for ease of use. By the 1980s, new owners had replaced the black slate with flagstone paving.

Lucite accessories, including the requisite cigarette boxes, lighters, and ashtrays, even though Elrod didn't smoke. The black glass–topped dining table matched with black leather and chrome sling chairs were placed next to the fireplace wall where the ceiling was lowest, and a trademark floating buffet hung below the clerestories. Each seating area focused on a different view of the desert and mountains.

But Elrod also introduced pieces by contemporary designers that intrigued him—Achille and Pier Giacomo Castiglioni's Arco lamp hanging over a group of Italian white leather chairs, Pierre Paulin's Ribbon Chairs in the same rust upholstery as the sofas, Warren Platner's nickel-plated steel rod chairs for Knoll in the bedroom, Danny Ho Fong for Tropi-Cal rattan chairs on the outdoor terrace. "When he was at his peak, the Pierre Paulin chairs were the coolest, the most avant-garde," says Brad Dunning. "He used the newest surfaces, lighting, fabrics. He was of the moment and not just designing for society people. A chair designed in Paris or Milan ended up in Palm Springs first because of him. He did a great service to the desert by making it international."

A mobile by Mimi Kornaza hovered above the sofas, a specially commissioned painting by Paul Jenkins was stretched on the curved courbaril wood wall that separated the living

"It's like living in a sculpture," Elrod said, "and that really is enough." In an early version of the interiors, a pair of Scandinavian birch armchairs sat in the center of the living room and Pierre Paulin's Ribbon chairs were grouped in the reading area. OPPOSITE: The intimate dining area, with black glass table and black leather and chrome chairs, was closest to the fireplace where the ceiling was at its lowest. Elrod designed the curved floating buffet that was fitted with stereo speakers.

LEFT: Stairs illuminated by lights covered with copper plates led down from the living room, between massive rock boulders, to the outdoor terrace and pool.

BOTTOM: The elliptical-shaped kitchen, partitioned behind the curved living room wall, with St. Charles cabinets, the upper ones faced in courbaril wood, the lower ones in gray plastic laminate, and black slate floor.

OPPOSITE: Elrod replaced the Scandinavian birch armchairs in the center of the living room with Ribbon chairs, and brought in four Italian leather armchairs for the reading area, which was illuminated by Achille and Pier Giacomo Castiglioni's Arco floor lamp, an oft-used lighting fixture in his projects. "A chair designed in Paris or Milan ended up in Palm Springs first because of him," says Los Angeles designer Brad Dunning. "He did a great service to the desert by making it international."

room from the kitchen. Works in the sculpture garden, grounds, and interiors were by Francisco Zúñiga, Harry Bertoia, Anthony Padovano, David Elder, and Gene Flores.

The master bedroom suite was a complete cocoon, a private world of rich reds, warm woods, carpets, cabinetry, recessed lighting, and every amenity for total relaxation. A row of interior walls with built-in bookshelves and closets were clad in a richly grained South American courbaril wood, the ceiling lined with limed redwood boards, and the wall-to-wall carpet was woven gray goat hair from Decorative Carpets. In the study/office area, delineated along the

windows by massive rock boulders, a deep daybed by Martin Brattrud covered in red and black textured fabric, red lacquered low tables, and a pair of Warren Platner chairs faced the fireplace. Beyond a glass and steel desk was a low room divider that contained bookshelves on the study side and became the headboard with shelves on the bed side. The king-size electric adjust-a-bed faced a mirrored wall hung with an Andy Nelson painting. So instead of facing out toward the panoramic view, Elrod's bed was positioned in the opposite direction, and the view was reflected in the mirror. As in most projects, Elrod had a master console next to his

OPPOSITE: A sitting area took up the first section of the master suite. Rich courbaril wood paneling covered the bedroom door and the inner walls that held shelving and built-in closets. Rough-sawn redwood boards were installed between the ceiling's concrete beams. By the fireplace were a pair of Warren Platner steel rod Easy Chairs and Ottoman for Knoll. Carpet was woven goat hair. BELOW: Facing out toward the massive boulders in the sitting area. Martin Brattrud daybed covered in textured Maria Kipp fabric, matching red lacquered side tables, Lightolier standing lamp, and plants that softened the perimeter around the rocks.

OPPOSITE: In the center of the master suite was a glass and steel desk and a low room divider with bookshelves of courbaril wood. The door at left led into the bathroom. BELOW: The other side of the room divider became the headboard, with the bed facing a smoked glass mirror wall on which hung an Andy Nelson painting. So the bed faced away from the view, which was reflected in the mirror. On the bedside shelf was a phone that connected to an intercom system, game of solitaire, phone and address book, notebook, small portable TV, and master panel switches that adjusted the bed and controlled the lights and music.

bed with push-button controls for raising and lowering the bed and dimming the lights and music, a telephone, and a portable television.

On the other side of the mirrored wall was the dressing area with a floor-to-ceiling closet of Lucite shelves for shirts and sweaters, a wet bar, and the bathroom suite. "I was interested in how he compartmentalized his clothes," says Katherine Hough. "Everything was arranged by color, style, and season. He had Chicago, Florida, and New York wardrobes. Everything was hung on beautiful chrome or steel hangers." The master bath contained a sauna, a massive five-foot-by-eight-foot shower, a custom sunken travertine whirlpool tub, and a freestanding vanity with an oval stainless steel sink, all screened off by a bamboo grove outside. The roof of the bedroom and carport was planted with a carpet of

yellow zinnias. Elrod purchased an acre of land below the house and began adding pockets of gardens. Hal Broderick said that Arthur was very friendly with the Native American people of the area. He bought the lot below his house from them and they allowed him to landscape it.

With its black slate floors and concrete cylinders recessed in the ceilings that held low-voltage downlighting, at night the house vanished and became one with the darkness.

Elrod now had a house that matched his aesthetic and reflected his interests. It was an arena where he could entertain friends, associates, clients, neighbors, and the press. Bob and Dolores Hope, who lived in a Spanish-style house in town, came for meetings every Thursday to discuss plans for their own John Lautner–designed house that would rise above Elrod's at the top of Southridge.

On the other side of the mirrored wall was the dressing area and master bath, complete with shower, sauna, sunken tub, wet bar, and exercise equipment. ABOVE: Reflected in the mirror where Elrod hung his bathrobe were the Lucite shelves that held his shirts and sweaters arranged by season. LEFT: Freestanding vanity with oval stainless sink and theatrical light bulbs around the mirror. OPPOSITE: Steps led down from the pool terrace to a series of trails with feeding stations for birds and wildlife. The pool was filled to the brim and overflowed down the concrete wall, a vanishing-edge technique of Lautner's.

Southridge In Print

The house debuted in print in the *Los Angeles Times Home* magazine on November 3, 1968. It was featured on the cover, a glorious composition in contrasting blues from the pool and grays from the concrete across the poolside terrace toward the elegantly flared column. The view beyond is of open desert and mountains, and two people—Mari Anne Pasqualetti and Bill Raiser—lean casually on the railing with their backs to the camera taking it all in. "It was about 115 degrees that morning, and we were trying to look relaxed!" said Mari Anne. Photographed by Richard Gross and written by *Home* magazine's associate editor Dan MacMasters, the feature titled "A Spectacular House That Grows Out of a Desert Ridge" presents the concrete structure as a striking, sculptural work of art and calls it "the ultimate Palm Springs house."

The combination of two well-regarded names in architecture and interior design who had produced a work of livable art proved catnip to magazine editors. Will Mehlhorn, the architecture editor at *House & Garden*, wrote to Lautner expressing interest in publishing the house.

In November 1968, architectural photographer Leland Y. Lee spent three days at the house with Will Mehlhorn, who had flown in from New York. "I had photographed one of Elrod's designs in Palm Springs before," recalled Leland Lee. "He told me he was going to build a new house. I thought, bachelor house with one room and a bathroom, something like

that. After the house was featured in the *Los Angeles Times*, a *House & Garden* editor called me and said, 'I want you to come pick me up at the Beverly Hills Hotel at the end of November and save me three days.' So we drive out, Mr. Mehlhorn, my assistant, and the station wagon loaded with all my equipment and two chrysanthemum topiaries I'd bought as a gift to help brighten the photos. The minute Elrod saw those topiaries he had his handyman take the van and he bought 20 more."

It was a seminal photo shoot, akin to Julius Shulman's 1947 session at Richard Neutra's Kaufmann House. Leland Lee had worked for Shulman as an assistant, and he used the same amount of precision and patience to get the

lighting just right and the shots he wanted. He insisted that the best exterior angles required a forklift, and so Elrod rented a cherry picker. This time, in the exterior photo of the rear façade, the two people barely visible at the edge of the upper terrace are Mari Anne Pasqualetti and Steve Chase. The house was featured in the May 1969 issue of *House & Garden* in a 10-page spread (but not the cover) titled "House Spectacular: Full of Daring Ideas." In a letter to Lautner, Mehlhorn later expressed his frustration with the page layouts and the use of more black-and-white photos than color. No matter. The two magazine features started an avalanche of press for the photogenic house, its architect, and, just as importantly, its client. *Architectural Digest, Palm Springs Life, Interior Design, Architectural Record* and countless other publications featured the home as a modern architectural wonder. Leland Lee's images ricocheted around the design world and are still referenced today. Arthur Elrod

had long shunned the spotlight, preferring to stay in the background, rarely photographed, rarely socializing with clients unless it was a charity event or housewarming party. This house changed everything. Overnight he became a celebrity and, in most cases, became better known than his clients. Mainstream publications like the influential newsweeklies *Time* and *Newsweek* included Elrod in their articles about home trends alongside such interior design heavyweights as Sister Parish, Billy Baldwin, and Francois Catroux. *Time* photographed Elrod sitting amid soap bubbles in his sunken tub as part of a feature titled "How the Other Half Bathes."

Still, for all the publicity and notoriety, Elrod preferred nothing more than getting up early, walking down the trails behind the house to watch the birds at the various feeding stations he'd set up, picking herbs to dry as potpourri, and enjoying the calm and peace of the desert at sunrise.

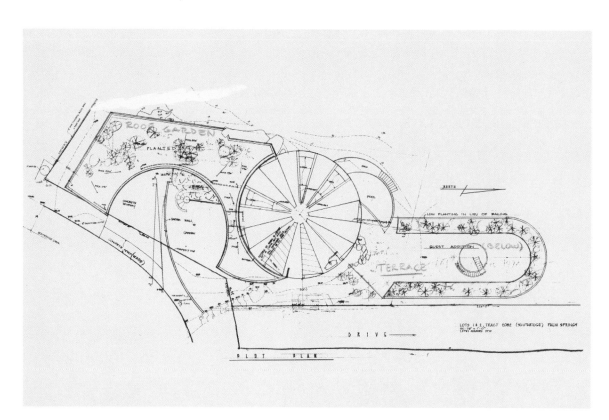

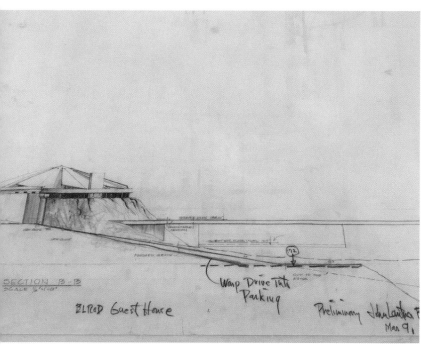

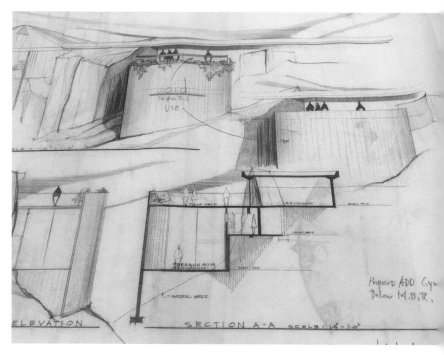

ABOVE: In 1970 Elrod purchased the adjacent lower lot and asked Lautner to design a 2,750-square-foot guest house that connected to the main house by extending the pool terrace. OPPOSITE: Around the same time, a windstorm blew in the mitered windows that wrapped around the living room. Lautner's solution was a massive retractable glass window that bisected the pool. To facilitate a clear path for the window, the flared support column was trimmed down to a rectangle.

In July 1970, Elrod purchased the adjacent lower Lot 1 (his three lots now totaled 2.96 acres) from Virginia Moore for $60,000 and he asked John Lautner to design an addition. In early 1971, Lautner drew up preliminary plans to extend the pool terrace and add a separate guest house with two bedrooms and a gym with its own carport lower down on Southridge, and by September had a complete set of revised plans. "Lautner was okay with going back and making adjustments," said Frank Escher. "He was always open to clients' input. He listened carefully and he respected them and they adored him. He almost made it into a game—how to translate his clients' requests into architecture." Alan Hess added, "He encouraged intelligent clients to be

involved. He wasn't averse to that at all. Lautner was never a historic preservationist. When he went back at the owner's request he was always interested, especially if new technology was available so that he could achieve what he wanted to achieve in a better way."

Around the same time in 1971 a freak windstorm blew in the mitered glass windows that zigzagged around the living room. "Doors flew off and the television set ended up in the middle of the Paul Jenkins artwork that had been specially stretched for the living room's arced wall," said Hal Broderick. "We were supposed to be having a party for a hundred just two weeks after the storm. We ended up edging the floor with potted plants so that people didn't step off the

engineering," said Alan Hess. "He consulted with an aerospace company to come up with the curved glass and hanging mechanism." Elrod wasn't concerned about the remodel—birds were constantly flying into the glass anyway. But some of the finesse of the original design was lost. "The revised plan cuts across the pool and would have interfered with the flared pier support, so to create a clear path for the sliding glass the column had to become a solid rectangle," says Frank Escher. "The roof was a piece of sculpture that seemed to float, now it's just a support. Once the renovation happened, there was a solid glass wall and no more overhang. Before, the transition went from covered indoors to covered outdoors to outdoors. The covered outdoors kept the heat away from the glass, and two of the skylights were open to the terrace. The original design made much more sense for the climate. An enormous a/c system had to be installed that turned the house into a greenhouse."

rocks and into the pool."

Frank Escher believed that the problem originated with the *Diamonds Are Forever* shoot. "The Bond film was clearly shot before the curved motorized glass wall was installed," he said. "You can see in the film clip that the skylights are open, there is no track for the motorized wall on the beam and, most importantly, the concrete column still has its elegant flare. All of that changed to accommodate the motorized wall. That means that the glass was removed for the filming and reinstalled, possibly incorrectly, which explains why it blew out in the storm."

Lautner replaced the mitered glass panels with a massive retractable glass curtain wall suspended from the roof's outer perimeter. "The glass wall was a major piece of

Not everything Elrod did at the house met with the neighbors' approval. According to the *Desert Sun*, "Speculation among some local flatland residents that a 'mausoleum' was being constructed atop exclusive Southridge on the south Palm Springs hillside was clarified today by the City Building Department" (January 19, 1973). The structure, it turned out, was a 15-foot-tall, 1,500-pound metal sculpture placed on top of the carport, and neighbors petitioned the city's planning department to have it removed.

The house played many roles—it was Elrod's private paradise, it was a party playground, it was his calling card. Shelter

magazine and society editors were invited up for lunches and barbecues where Elrod manned the grill. Clients were always calling and stopping by. When Bill Blass came to town for a fashion show in February 1973, Elrod hosted a celebrity-packed dinner party chronicled by the *Desert Sun*. Elizabeth Taylor and Richard Burton supposedly stopped by. William Holden and Steve McQueen were neighbors. "Arthur wanted a party house, and he got one," said Hal Broderick. The parties continued and became legendary. Elrod's New Year's Eve parties were a highlight of the social calendar.

In November 1971, *Playboy* ran a feature aptly titled "A Playboy Pad: Pleasure on the Rocks" and, in the bachelor pad lingo of the times, refers to it as a "pad" or "digs," not as a "home." The Elrod House embodied the myth of the ultimate bachelor pad even more than the Playboy Mansion—it was cool and progressive and photogenic at the same time. "Southridge is the sexiest bachelor pad in the U.S., if not the world," said Brad Dunning. "It is the definitive bachelor pad."

Arthur Elrod had arrived!

The Elrod house was immortalized in *Diamonds Are Forever,* which filmed there in 1970. Some props were brought in (trapeze, breakaway plastic coffee table, plastic posts), but most of the furnishings are visible in the scene. Here Sean Connery (James Bond) and Trina Parks (Thumper) wait between takes on Gaetano Pesce's Up chair and ottoman and the Martin Brattrud arced sofa.

Diamonds Are Forever, 1971

The house lives on forever because of the memorable sequence in the James Bond film *Diamonds Are Forever.* In it, James Bond (played by Sean Connery) is searching for reclusive billionaire Willard Whyte (a character loosely based on Howard Hughes and played by Jimmy Dean, country music singer, TV host, and, yes, the sausage king), who is being held captive in his summer house supposedly outside Las Vegas and guarded by Bambi and Thumper.

"I wanted to look at exotic-looking places in Palm Springs and I was shown the Elrod house and it was absolutely right for the film," related production designer Ken Adam about the location scouting. "It was a reinforced concrete structure, very modern and fabulous. I said, 'This is as though I designed it. I don't have to do anything.'" But, according to Adam, Elrod was reluctant to have his home invaded by the filmmakers. So Adam called producer Albert "Cubby" Broccoli, who was very close to Beverly Hills labor lawyer and "fixer" for the Chicago mob, Sidney Korshak, who had a vacation house in Palm Springs. "Cubby rang Sidney and within half an hour we had the house," Adam recounted. An apocryphal story, perhaps, but an irresistible part of the home's lore.

In this particular scene, James Bond and his CIA counterpart Felix Leiter pull up below the house, which is visible atop a steep rocky slope. Bond, jacket slung over one shoulder, then appears around the outside curved motor-court wall, pushes open the copper entry gate and walks down the path toward the glass front door. He opens the door and is greeted inside the living room by Bambi in a Gaetano Pesce chair and bikini-clad Thumper, who is reclining on top of a rock. There's an ensuing fight before they push Bond into the pool just below the living room and dive in after him. Apart from some props, the original furnishings and art, including the Paul Jenkins painting, Pierre Paulin's Ribbon chairs, and the Martin Brattrud arced sofa, are visible in the background.

"We filmed the scene at the house in 1970—it was one of the last scenes that they shot," recalled Trina Parks, who played Thumper. "It took us about two weeks because we rehearsed it like real theater. The entire scene is only about three and a half minutes long, but each section had a scene change with a different cameraman—for example, when Sean comes in by himself and brings me down took a whole day. The first couple of days were just us, Sean, director Guy Hamilton, producer Cubby Broccoli, and the stuntman. We rehearsed what we were going to do that day, what the scene was about, each step—when I come down off the rock, how is he bringing me down, all tightly choreographed like a fight scene today, but without any digital effects.

"I'd never seen a house like that. It was amazing to see a house built right out of the rocks. They brought in very few things—plastic posts, a breakaway plastic coffee table, and a trapeze hanging from the ceiling—but everything else was original. When you walk in you see the rock on the left and the living room in front of you with the view. I couldn't figure out where the kitchen was—it was behind the wall where I do flips. My dressing room was the master bedroom—one very large oblong room. Everything was very square and pointed in that house, nothing fancy, just neat and sharp."

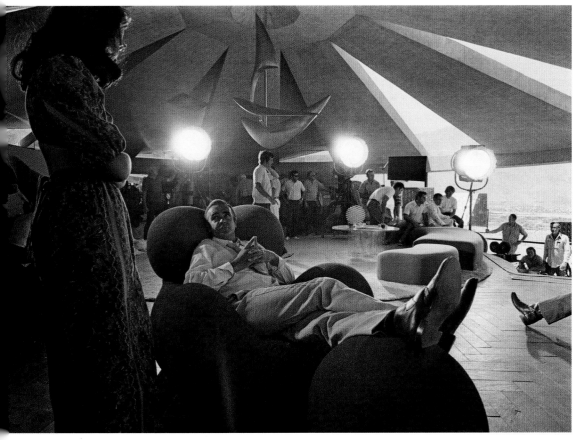

Early on the morning of Monday, February 18, 1974, Arthur Elrod and William Raiser left the house on Southridge and headed as usual to the studio in Raiser's blue Fiat convertible. Elrod didn't drive—he had lost his license countless times for speeding and he never wore a seat belt. Around 7:50 A.M. their car was broadsided by a pickup truck driven by a teenager who ran a red light at high speed at the intersection of Farrell Drive and Ramon Road. The teenager was later charged with felony drunk driving.

Both men died at the scene. Bill Raiser was 58. Arthur Elrod was 49.

The obituary notices that ran locally and nationally in newspapers including the *Desert Sun, Los Angeles Times,* and *New York Times,* expressed the shock and disbelief at their sudden deaths.

Arthur Elrod was cremated in a private service. There was no memorial. Out of respect for their mother, Jessie, Sam Calloway placed a grave marker in the cemetery of the Flat Rock Baptist Church in Anderson, South Carolina, that says simply Arthur D., Jr. 1923–1974. The Faculty Women's Club of the College of the Desert announced in March that an annual Elrod-Raiser Scholarship would be awarded to a student in the Art Department.

On April 21, 1974, the *Los Angeles Times Home* magazine, which had been such an early and loyal supporter of his work, printed a two-page tribute titled "The Life and Happy Times of Arthur Elrod" by associate editor Dan MacMasters that included quotes from many friends and collaborators in the industry:

Arthur had tremendous enthusiasm but at the same time he could concentrate on the business at hand and get things done. This was great for everyone on a project. But there was more than that. My relationship with him was exceptional. He was everything a client should be. He had an understanding of architecture and he was always open to new ideas. He never

wanted to do the safe thing. He accepted my design and my recommendations entirely, and there was no interference. I think he was still maturing and developing when he died.

—*John Lautner*

He really believed in people, but as individuals. One afternoon at his house he must have talked two hours about that. This is the age of the individual, he told me. He felt that Home *and other shelter magazines were too impersonal, that we should be reflecting how people lived and thought.*

—*James Toland, editor,*
Los Angeles Times Home *magazine*

If a client called from Chicago in the afternoon with a problem, Arthur might be on a plane east that night. He had practically no social life outside his business, and his idea of a dinner was a hamburger in a taxi on the way to the airport. Arthur had many things going for him—good looks, immense personal charm and talent—but he never let them substitute for hard work. No detail was too small to attend to. He did many designs for Home *magazine. Often he would spend thousands of dollars of his own money to get the look he wanted, the Arthur Elrod look. When it came time for photographing, Arthur would have a truckload of accessories literally standing by for use.*

—*Barbara Lenox, longtime*
Los Angeles Times Home *magazine contributor*

Arthur was a designer's designer, both in his ethics and the quality of his work. I was head of the AID in those expanding years and Arthur was one of the young people who did so much to help it grow. He contributed greatly to its professionalism, and many of our people grew in his reflection. Arthur had a gift for a subtle kind of opulence that avoided the ostentatious. And he had style.

—*Adele Faulkner,*
past president of the Association of Interior Designers

You always remembered when you first met Arthur, for he made you feel as though you had just been discovered. One of the last times I saw him was equally memorable. Leland Lee and I had been photographing at his house and we stayed on for dinner, relaxing with good food and watching the incomparable nightfall on the desert. Then midway through the meal some clients arrived and Arthur left to show them around. It was rather like dining in an airport lounge. Soon after dinner he excused himself to run down to the studio for a while . . . In 1973 he told Babara Lenox that he had grossed a million dollars. What made Arthur run? The Success Ethic? An ego trip? Dollars and more dollars? Perhaps something of all these, and perhaps none of them at all. He had it made. He certainly didn't need the money or the recognition. And if Arthur had an ego, you never knew it. Perhaps it was just something as basic as his love for people, his consuming need for people. He was like a bright and joyous mirror into which you looked and were happy. But beyond it you could not see. In the last year or two he would confess to close friends that he was weary. He wanted nothing more than to go home to his ridgetop and feed his birds and look out across the desert. And we didn't believe that. Now it doesn't matter. He was an original and will not come our way again. God speed you, Arthur Elrod.

—Dan MacMasters, associate editor,
Los Angeles Times Home *magazine*

I had admired Arthur's designs since I was 17, and working with him fulfilled one of my early dreams. Arthur had great organizational abilities. He taught me how to approach my work, how to achieve order. And I have a reverence for order in my work now. He knew how to give people an environment that was right for them, how not to impose his own personality. Oh, he was an independent with plenty of spirit, but he was no prima donna. He never disliked anyone, but he avoided the social aspects of working with clients, like cocktail parties, as I have chosen to do also. Arthur died suddenly and violently, and as often happens, it's taken years to absorb his absence.

Often a strange phenomena occurs. If I'm working during a desert storm and hear a clap of thunder, I am overwhelmed by his presence. I know he is there. It's rather an intermittent reminder of his impact.

—Steve Chase, Q&A with Sharon Apfelbaum,
Palm Springs Life, *October 1980*

Arthur departed us in a tragic auto accident in February 1974, and the firm, the design industry and his loyal and devoted clients felt the loss for many years after. A career that had not reached its pinnacle, but a talent so solid and innovative it still inspires the design world today.

—Marybeth Norton Waterman

Elrod had taken his nephew Michael Calloway under his wing, and starting in 1962 Michael came out to Palm Springs for the summer, staying with Elrod, assisting in the studio and traveling with him to various jobs. Michael credits his uncle with giving him the impetus to leave the South:

One day in 1971—I was in my 20s, and it was the last time I was with him—I asked why he left South Carolina. He said, "I had to get away from home." I knew what he meant. He helped me leave.

—Michael Calloway

Arthur Elrod's Legacy

Hal Broderick and Steve Chase didn't particularly like each other, but they kept the firm running and completed the projects that Elrod and Raiser had been working on, which included Sigmund Edelstone's condo at the Racquet Club. "We all work so closely together that most of us are familiar with each other's projects," Steve Chase told *Interior Design* in 1974.

The exception was the $3.5 million Hope House at the top of Southridge, on which construction had stopped in July 1973 after a fire destroyed the central roof's wood framing and damaged the steel girders. Work restarted in 1977 but by that point Elrod was gone, John Lautner had grown frustrated with the Hopes' constant changes, and the dream of what could have been never materialized until now. Ron Burkle, who once owned the Elrod House, purchased the Hope House in 2016 for $13 million. He is working on a major restoration with architect and longtime Lautner associate Helena Arahuete, who says she is "taking the house back to its original design, to the way Mr. Lautner would have wanted it." Elrod was also working with Lautner on Marbrisa in Acapulco and had completed furnishings, some of which (a distinctive floating buffet with a striking geometric motif on the front, for example) are still in place.

Steve Chase left in 1980 to open his own interior design practice in Rancho Mirage, which would become hugely successful. He was seen as the heir apparent to Elrod—his polished interiors also exploded with layers of color and texture; he was also a major collector of contemporary art, and his clients also commissioned multiple residences. The majority of his projects were featured in *Architectural Digest.* Chase died in 1994 and donated his 132-piece art collection to the Palm Springs Art Museum plus $1.5 million toward building a wing to house it. The Steve Chase Art Wing, designed by E. Stewart Williams, opened in 1996.

Hal Broderick kept Arthur Elrod Associates running and continued on with his own clients, notably actress Mary Martin. In 1976, he and friends of Elrod's contributed funds to create the Arthur Elrod Sculpture Garden at the Palm Springs Desert Museum. In 1996, Hal and his partner Cal Vander Woude retired to Sonoma. Hal passed away in 2006. After his death, Cal donated the firm's archives to the Palm Springs Art Museum's Architecture and Design Center.

As the executor of Elrod's estate, Broderick put the Elrod House on Southridge on the market a few months after Elrod's death and it sold in November 1974 to Steve and Patricia Maloney for $1.5 million. "I saw the house in *Architectural Digest* and called Arthur Elrod's office and found out he'd recently died in a car crash and his house was going to

be sold," says Steve Maloney. "We bought it sight unseen—we were blown away by its contemporary design, uniqueness, and the use of materials." The Maloneys purchased the house completely furnished. The 34-page household inventory runs the gamut from every single piece of furniture in every room to the art (appraised at around $90,000) to every tabletop accessory, all china, glass, and silverware, kitchen utensils, bathroom accessories, linens, exercise equipment, planters, everything down to Elrod's books, which were mostly about art.

In 1977, the Maloneys asked John Lautner to draw up plans for another addition that extended further over Lot 1. "We felt that the idea of a library, larger pool, and tennis court would be a great addition to the property," says Steve Maloney. He grew up in Kalamazoo, Michigan, with an appreciation for great architecture, especially the work of Frank Lloyd Wright, and he recognized Wright's influences in Lautner's work. As a child he had been a frequent visitor to Palm Springs—his grandparents Donald and Genevieve Gilmore wintered at Smoke Tree Ranch in their Albert Frey–designed house, which had been decorated by Elrod in 1958, and Maloney remembers meeting Frey at their home. The Maloneys met on-site with Lautner, who was also from Michigan. "I liked John because he was easygoing, very engaged, pure, and focused on his architecture," says Steve Maloney. But after seven years the couple, who had three children, grew tired of the home's maintenance, and the plans were never executed.

The Maloneys listed the house on June 24, 1979, with most of the original furniture still intact for $2.7 million. It sold in January 1980 to Dr. Borko Djordjevic and his wife, Geneva, for $985,000. Lautner provided the same drawings for a pool and tennis court for the Djordjevics in 1981. He also drew up plans for alterations and additions to the master bath and dressing area. Neither was carried out, but many other changes were made without his input. Most of the furnishings were removed or reupholstered, the center of the living room's slate floor was replaced with parquet, the kitchen plastic laminate countertops were replaced with tile, and a mirrored ceiling was added in the bedroom.

Sotheby Parke-Bernet marketed the house under the name of "Sunburst" and offered it for sale for $10 million. Djordjevic lost the house in a trustee sale in 1989 after it had been listed for sale for several years, with the price drifting steadily south to $1.8 million. A 1993 remodel by Oklahoma oilman Ward S. Merrick III saw the St. Charles kitchen cabinets torn out, the kitchen's wood paneling stuccoed over, and the roof's two open clerestories enclosed with heavy ribbed glass. "The house had been bastardized starting in the '80s," says Frank Escher. "It became diametrically opposed to what the house was about."

Ron Burkle bought the house in 1995 for $1.3 million. The supermarket magnate, investor, philanthropist, and architecture aficionado brought in his designer Steve Heisler to undertake a major restoration and deal with delayed maintenance issues. Burkle never spent a night there, but he allowed the house to be photographed in 1998 for the book *Palm Springs Modern*. "I love architecture," he told Janice Kleinschmidt in *Palm Springs Life*, May 1, 2017. "And when I see something that I have known or admired or think is amazing and it is in bad condition, I enjoy buying it and putting it back to where it looks like it once did—or closer to the architect's intent than it ended up. I always thought Frank Lloyd Wright and John Lautner were architects with whom everybody connected," said Burkle, who now owns the Hope House on Southridge and their long-time residence in Toluca Lake. "The Elrod House was in a state of disrepair when I bought it. I never had any intention of living there; I bought it for its beauty."

Burkle sold the Elrod House in November 2003 to developer and real estate investor Michael Kilroy for $5.5 million. Kilroy purchased two other houses on Southridge but lost all three to Lloyds Bank in foreclosure in 2016.

The house is currently undergoing a major restoration by Los Angeles architect Mark Haddawy for its current owner, fashion designer Jeremy Scott, who purchased the house for $7.700 million (a nice reworking of 007) in 2016.

On February 12, 2005, the Architecture and Design Council of the Palm Springs Art Museum held a one-day symposium titled "Design in the Desert: Arthur Elrod." Organized by Sidney Williams and Katherine Hough, the event featured keynote speeches by Paige Rense-Noland, then editor in chief of *Architectural Digest* now editor emeritus, and Hal Broderick. A panel moderated by Modern Way owner Courtney Newman with photographer Leland Lee, furniture designer Charles Hollis Jones, and designer Brad Dunning discussed the firm and its place in the design world. The day also included a tour of some of Elrod's existing projects, and it was because of this symposium that Hal Broderick compiled the chronological list of the firm's projects.

Elrod left very little in the way of personal documents. He was famously reticent about revealing much about himself, and except for one handwritten letter and signed guest books in the archive there is nothing that gives any insight to his personal life. He poured all of his energy and emotions into his work. Hal Broderick presumably threw out whatever personal papers were in the house when it was sold, but he did keep everything to do with the firm for his oft-promised memoir, which he sadly never wrote. Those records form the basis for the Arthur Elrod Associates archive at the Palm Springs Art Museum's Architecture and Design Center and for this book. Broderick and Chase received all credit for the projects that were published after February 1974. Elrod's sole legacy until now resided in the global fascination with the Elrod House on Southridge, a fascination that has continued unabated for 50 years.

I hope this book helps restore the luster to Arthur Elrod's remarkable trajectory, which saw a boy born on a farm in South Carolina reach for the stars and firmly stick his landing.

The firm completed hundreds of projects, large and small, residential and commercial, spec houses, model homes, and designer showhouses. Hal Broderick researched and compiled this project list for the Architecture and Design Council Symposium titled "Design in the Desert: Arthur Elrod" at the Annenberg Theater of the Palm Springs Art Museum on February 12, 2005. This list is neither exhaustive nor definitive—many minor projects were omitted and the archive contains countless index cards that are impossible to categorize. Every effort has been made to update the chronology with relevant details—wives' first names, street addresses, architect, publication dates, clients' professions. Any additional information or inaccuracies will be corrected in future editions.

Abbreviations:

CC = Country Club
LA = Los Angeles
PD = Palm Desert
PS = Palm Springs
RM = Rancho Mirage
M/M = Mr./Mrs. where I have been unable to determine the wife's first name

The design work originating through the workshops of Arthur Elrod Associates is most unique in several ways, not least for its duration and high level of excellence. The 'catalogue raisonné' of projects that follows provides an impressive list of examples of the high quality, professionalism and future-sighted vision that was always a central and unifying core of the work produced. This is quite evident in both the obvious satisfaction of the clients by returning to the firm for multiple contracts and multiple generations but also by the number of celebrities that chose the firm and its designers.

—Harold C. Broderick, ASID

1940s

Assorted projects while working at Bullock's Palm Springs
Model home in Vista Del Cielo tract on East Ramon built by the R. H. Grant Construction Company/Sunny Dunes Development Corp.
Samuel and Betty Friedberg, 710 Paseo De Anza, PS

1948

Russell and Molvine Denney, 1585 South Calle Marcus, Deepwell Estates, PS

1952-54

Diamond Jubilee of Light, San Francisco Museum of Art
Assorted projects while working at W. & J. Sloane, San Francisco
M/M Harry Reid, Diablo CC, Diablo CA

1954

Arthur Elrod Ltd., 886 N. Palm Canyon Dr., PS
Lucille Ball and Desi Arnaz, 40–241 Club View Dr., Thunderbird CC, RM. Paul R. Williams architect
Bow and Nancy Herbert, 976 Avenida Palos Verdes, PS. Owner, Horseshoe Club and the Gardena Club, Gardena
Joseph and Joyce Pawling, 231 Lilliana Dr., PS. Wexler & Harrison architects. *LA Times Home,* Jan. 16, 1955. Contractor

1955

Arthur Elrod, 419 Valmonte Sur, PS. Adobe house purchased from Frank and Melba Bennett. House #1. *LA Times Home,* Jan. 29, 1961
Hal Broderick, 330 Mariscal Rd., PS. House #1
Melba and Frank Bennett, El Sueno, 1184 Camino Mirasol, PS. *LA Times Home,* Jan 1, 1956

Hyman C. Berkowitz, Sand Springs Ranch, Wendell, Idaho. *Desert Sun* Aug. 4, 1955, *PS Villager,* Sept. 1955. President, Old Mr. Boston Distillers
William Boggess, 1366 Calle de Maria, PS. Wexler & Harrison architects, Joe Pawling builder, Cactus Slim Moorten landscape design. *LA Times Home,* Jan. 1, 1956. Realtor
M/M H.S. Bonesteel Jr., Atherton, CA
Hoagy Carmichael, 40–267 Club View Dr., Thunderbird CC, RM. William F. Cody alterations
Edwin J. Heimer, Santa Elena, PS. House #1
Laurena Heple, 1050 N. Cahuilla Road, PS. Project #1
Edwin H. "Buddy" and Carolyn Morris, 650 N. Via Miraleste, PS. John Porter Clark architect, former Alice Guthrie house, 1939. Music publisher, head of ASCAP. *PS Villager,* May 1955. House #1

Desert Braemar, Display Models, 100 N. Palm Canyon Drive, PS

1956

Arthur Elrod, 140 Via Lola (while Valmonte Sur was being renovated), PS
Barney and Loie Adelaar, 666 Mel Ave., PS. Adelaar Bros., NY
Georgia and Paul Aust, 296 Hermosa Place, PS. Realtor
Lucille Ball and Desi Arnaz, 1000 N. Roxbury Dr., Beverly Hills
Charles and Winifred Becker, 828 Avenida Palos Verdes, PS. Franklin Life Insurance
"Home of Tomorrow," 295 Hermosa Place, Las Palmas, PS. Spec house built by Joe Pawling. *Palm Springs Villager,* Dec. 1956. Sold in 1957 to Victor and Danielle Nemeroff for $250,000. Chairman, Allied Paper Co. Sold in 1961 to Edie and Lew Wasserman. Head of MCA
Mary Hurrell, 374 Vereda del Sur, PS
Culver and Sallie Nichols, 1120 Paseo El Mirador, PS. Clark, Frey, Chambers architects, Ken Nishimoto landscape architect. *PS Villager,* Oct. 1956

CHRONOLOGY OF SELECTED PROJECTS
OF ARTHUR ELROD ASSOCIATES

Ed and Bertha Robbin, 1120 Alejo Road, PS. Herbert Burns architectural designer, 1948. Former spec house built by developer Fay Brainard. *Palm Springs Villager*, Sept. 1956

Lucy and Claude Simpson, 1111 Tamarisk Road, PS

Glenn and Dorothy Wallichs, Beverly Hills. Cofounder Capitol Records, Wallichs Music City, Hollywood

Harold Hicks Real Estate, 1345 N. Palm Canyon Dr., PS. Williams, Williams & Williams architects

Reading Room, First Church of Christ Scientist, 373 S. Palm Canyon Drive, PS

7th Annual Decorators and Antique Show, Pan-Pacific Auditorium, LA

1957

Arthur Elrod, 350 Via Lola, Las Palmas, PS. House #2. Sold fully furnished in 1964 to the Hamlings. *Palm Springs Life*, Aug. 1962. *Architectural Digest*, Winter 1963 (Vol. XIX, No. 4). *Interior Design*, Aug. 1963, *LA Times*, Oct. 13, 1963

M/M Isaac (Ike) Baron, Arcadia, CA

Elsie Peiser and George L. Bond, 127 Isabella, Atherton, CA. President, Stauffer Chemical

John S. Campbell, 1415 Ocotillo Ave., PS. Founder Malt-O-Meal Co.

Sydney and Rachel Charney, 37–127 Marx Circle, Tamarisk CC, RM. Wexler & Harrison architects. Eckbo, Royston & Williams landscape. *LA Times Home*, June 9, 1957. *Palm Springs Life*, Oct. 3, 1958 [Vol. 1, No. 10]. Attorney

Marion Davies, Desert Inn remodel, 153 N. Palm Canyon Dr., PS

Walt and Lillian Disney, Smoke Tree Ranch, PS. Carl W. Denney, architect

Myron E. Glass, Desert Braemar #33, 69–580 Hwy 111, Cathedral City

Pearl Helms, Smoke Tree Ranch, PS. Widow of Paul Helms, Helms Bakery

Edwin J. and Georgia Heimer, 1133 Buena Vista, PS. House #2

Laurena Heple and Walt Bratney, 17 Mile Dr., Pebble Beach. *LA Times Home*, Dec. 28, 1958. Project #2

Harold Hicks, 395 Camino Norte, PS

H. Barkley Johnson, Thunderbird CC, RM

Thea and Leon Koerner, 1275 Calle de Maria, PS, Stewart Williams architect, Eckbo, Royston & Williams landscape architects. Founder Alaska Pine Co.

E. Phillip Lyon, 993 N. Patencio Rd., PS

George Murphy, Smoke Tree Ranch, PS. Actor/politician

Victor and Danielle Nemeroff, 295 Hermosa Place, PS. Chairman, Allied Paper Co., Chicago. Former "Home of Tomorrow"

Jacqueline Cochran Odlum, Cochran-Odlum Ranch, Indio. Aviatrix

Edward and Edna Small, 467 Via Lola, PS. Film producer

Norman and Peg Waters, 280 Vereda Sur, PS. Date grower

Marco Wolff, 1837 Caliente Road, PS

First Church of Christ, Scientist, Palm Springs, 605 Riverside Dr. South, PS. Albert Frey and Robson Chambers, architects

Desert Braemar Model Homes, 100 N. Palm Canyon Dr., PS

Royal Air Country Club Apartments, 389 W. Tahquitz Drive (site that once belonged to the Desert Inn Mashie Golf Course). Wexler & Harrison architects, Antone Dalu landscaping. Model units

AAUW (American Association of University Women), Palm Springs Chapter, 1st Annual Home Tour, Feb. 3, 1957. Homes of Ed and Bertha Robbin, 1120 Alejo; Bill Boggess, 1366 Calle de Maria

8th Annual Decorators and Antique Show, Pan-Pacific Auditorium, LA. White and gold bedroom. *LA Times*, Oct. 11, 1957, *House Beautiful*, March 1958

1958

Albert and Gertrude Baskin, 1093 La Jolla, PS

Saul and Joan Cogen, 1001 Norman Place, LA

Claudette Colbert, 1255 Camino Mirasol, PS

Tom and Dottie Davis, 70–378 Pecos Road, Thunderbird Heights, RM. Eggers & Wilkman architects. T. H. Robsjohn-Gibbings interiors

Donald and Genevieve Gilmore, Smoke Tree Ranch, PS. Albert Frey architect. Chairman of the Board, Upjohn Company, founder Gilmore Car Museum

Marie E. Green, Rancho Santa Fe, CA. *LA Times*, Aug. 24, 1958

H. Barkley Johnson, Malibu. House #2

Emil and Ruth Laufer, 423 Merito Place, PS, Richard Harrison architect

Ann Peppers, Heather Downs, Route #1, Mentone, CA. *LA Times Home*, March 1, 1959

Gladys Stroud, 1991 Yucca Place, PS. Project #1

Theodore and Marguerite Sutter, 1207 Calle de Maria, PS. Stewart Williams architect. CEO Baker Oil Tools Co.

Racquet Club Road Estates, 289 Racquet Club Road and 325 Francis Dr., PS. Alexander Construction Co., Palmer & Krisel architects, landscape design Don Crabtree. Model homes

Mountain View Estates, 615 N. Via Monte Vista, PS. George Alexander Co. Charles E. DuBois architect. Model home

Vista Las Palmas Estates, 1132 Vista Vespero, PS. Model home

Los Angeles Times Home magazine house, Royal Highlands, Encino, Edward Fickett architect. Residence of James Toland, editor of *Home* magazine

Palm Lanes Estates, 264 Debby Dr., PS. Builder Jack Meiselman. Model home

Enchanted Homes, 202 Louella Road, PS. Model home

2nd Annual AAUW home tour. Frank and Melba Bennett home, 1184 Camino Mirasol. Elrod was the only designer's work represented.

9th Annual Decorator's Show, Los Angeles, 1958. Dining room and music area. *LA Times*, Oct. 5, 1958

1959

Elrod spec house, Smoke Tree Ranch, PS
Hal Broderick, 154 San Antonio Dr., PS. House #2
Ernest and Leonore Alschuler, 425 Via Lola, PS. President Erla-Sentinel Radio Corp., Evanston, Ill. Lapham and Iwata architects. Sold to Henry and Nancy Ittleson, then to Sidney and Alexandra Sheldon
Hazel Fairless, 561 Camino Norte, PS. Ex-wife of Ben Fairless, president of U.S. Steel. House #1
Meyer and Jean Gensburg, 1509 Manzanita, PS. Cofounder of Genco arcade game machines, real estate investor
Birdie Lyman, 829 N. Patencio, PS. Widow of L.A. restaurateur Mike Lyman. Built by Jack Kenaston in 1937, purchased by the Lymans in 1948, remodeled in June '59 by Stewart Williams. *Palm Springs Life*, April 1962
Ralph Ogden, 70–340 Placerville Road, Thunderbird CC, RM
Frankie and Edward Pfeffer, 700 W. Stevens Road, PS
M/M Len Weissman, 2316 Donella Circle, West LA. Ed Fickett architect, Lee Lauger builder, Albert Heinemann landscape architect. *LA Times Home*, Oct. 18, 1959

Eldorado Country Club Clubhouse, Indian Wells. William F. Cody and Stanley Smith, architects. *Palm Springs Life*, Dec. 1960
Eldorado Palms Estates, Indian Wells. Model Home
Golden Vista Estates, 963 Via Monte Vista, PS. Alexander Construction Company. Model home
Vista Las Palmas, 700 Via Las Palmas, 1215 Via Paraiso and 1320 Granito Circle, George Alexander Co. Palmer & Krisel architects. Model homes
Palm Lane Estates, 217 Michelle Road, PS. Model home
The Hideaway, Ethel Strebe and John Harutun, Deep Well Ranch, 1020 E. Palm Canyon Dr., PS

Japanese Teahouse, Pan-Pacific Auditorium, Decorators + Antique Show. *LA Times Home*, Oct. 11, 1959

1960

Charles Clare, 71–088 Fairway Dr., Tamarisk CC, RM. William Cody architect
Barney and Emma Dagan, 215 Harford Place, Upland
Sidney and Fanny Feuchtwanger, 417 W. Camino Road, PS
Samuel and Hermine Greenfield, 853 N. Patencio, PS
Thomas and Lynn Starr Hull, 1350 Manzanita, PS. *Palm Springs Life*, June/July 1960
Robert and Marianne Leaver, Palisades Dr., PS. Hugh Kaptur architect. *LA Times*, Sept. 8, 1963
Maurice and Ruth Melamed, 885 W. Ferndale Road, Wayzata, MN. *Architectural Digest*, Fall 1962 (Vol. XIX, No. 3). Cofounder Coast to Coast stores
Ray and Doris Mithun, Wayzata, MN
Richard and Helen Snideman, 40–140 Paseo Grande, Thunderbird CC, RM. House #1
Joan Winchell, Bermuda Dunes Country Club. *LA Times* columnist

1961

Hal Broderick, 2652 Starr Road, Racquet Club Road Estates, PS. House #3
Malcolm and Adeline Clarke, 272 N. Via Las Palmas, PS
Moss and Kitty Carlisle Hart, 467 Via Lola, PS (former owner Eddie Small)
Laurence Harvey, 9274 Swallow Dr., LA. Buff & Hensman architects. House #2
Ann Peppers, 49380 Avenida Fernando, La Quinta. A. Quincy Jones architect. Project #2

1st Annual Palm Springs Decorators & Antique Show and Sale, Palm Springs Playhouse. Lanai Room
Art Show, NCJW and AID, Sunset Room, Ambassador Hotel, Los Angeles

Ethel's Hideaway, Ethel Strebe and John Harutun, Smoke Tree Center, PS
Eldorado Country Club Cottages West, William Cody architect
Virginia and Holmes Tuttle (auto dealer and Reagan intimate)
Pat and Randolph Scott (actor)
Leonard and Polly Firestone (businessman/ambassador)
M/M Richard R. Nelson
Racquet Club Road Estates, 289 Racquet Club Road, 2745 Kitty Hawk Dr. and 2792 Avenida Caballeros. Alexander Construction Co., Palmer and Krisel architects. *LA Times Home*, March 19, 1961. Model homes

1962

Laurena Heple, 1430 Sunset Plaza Dr., L.A. Project #3
Eugene V. and Frances Klein, 410 Trousdale Place, Beverly Hills. William R. Stephenson architect, Jocelyn Domela landscape design. *Architectural Digest*, Spring 1963; *Time* magazine, Feb. 9, 1968
Edwin (Buddy) H. Morris Music Publishing Co., 31 W. 54th St., New York. Project #2
Richard and Helen Snideman, Pebble Beach. House #2
Louise and Lionel Steinberg, 797 Via Vadera, PS. House #1
M/M Marco Wolff, 9515 Heather Road, Beverly Hills

Calcor/Rheem Prefabricated Steel Houses, Alexander Construction Co., Wexler & Harrison architects. Model Home #1, 290 E. Simms Road; Model Home #2, 3125 N. Sunny View Dr.; Model Home #3, 3100 N. Sunny View Dr. *LA Times Home*, May 13, 1962, *Home Builders Journal*, Aug. 1962, *Architectural Record*, May 1963
Los Angeles Times Home magazine house, Yorba Linda Country Club. Richard Dorman architect. *LA Times Home*, June 24, 1962

Racquet Club Road Estates, 1115 Padua
Way, PS. Model home
2nd Annual Palm Springs Decorators and
Antique Show, Palm Springs Pavilion,
401 S. Pavilion Way, PS
6th Annual AAUW home tour. Arthur
Elrod home, 350 Via Lola, PS

1963

Fay and Welton Becket, Eldorado Country
Club, Indian Wells
George R. and Anne McNab Bond, 143
Isabella Ave., Atherton, CA
Doris and Louis Factor, 804 N. Elm Dr.,
Beverly Hills
Jack and Loras Fascinato, 956 San Loren-
zo, PS. Composer, arranger, songwriter,
music director for Tennessee Ernie
Ford, composer "Palm Springs Suite"
John Frankenheimer, Malibu Colony, Mali-
bu. Director
Meyer and Jean Gensburg, 1108 Wallace
Ridge Road, Beverly Hills. House #2.
Cofounder with brothers of Genco coin
and arcade game machines
Laurena Heple, Diamond Head Apart-
ments, 2969 Kalakaua Ave., Honolulu,
Hawaii. Vladimir Ossipoff architect. Proj-
ect #4. *Desert Sun*, Mar. 31, 1966
Asher and Marie Levy, 375 Hermosa Place,
PS
Nelda and Joe Linsk, 470 W. Vista Chino,
PS (Kaufmann House, Richard Neutra
architect). Addition of family room and
office, architect William Cody. Project #1
Edwin "Buddy" and Carolyn Morris, 2320
Cantina Way, PS. Project #3
Ann Peppers, 10333 Wilshire Blvd. #17D,
LA. Project #3
Gladys Stroud, 10333 Wilshire Blvd., #16A,
LA. Project #2

Golf Club Estates, 2119 Birdie Way, PS.
Alexander Construction Co.
Reeves Towers, 137 S. Reeves Dr., Beverly
Hills. "First Prestige Steel and Concrete
High Rise Residence." Model unit
Spalding Towers, 330 S. Spalding Dr., LA.
Model unit
3rd Annual Palm Springs Decorators and

Antique Show, Palm Springs Pavilion,
401 S. Pavilion Way, PS
Outdoor Pavilion, World Garden and
Flower Show, Pan-Pacific Auditorium,
LA Times Home magazine.

1964

William C. Raiser joins Arthur Elrod
Associates
Waldo and Alice Avery, 355 W. Vereda Sur,
PS. William Cody architect
Arthur E. and I'lee Bailey, Smoke Tree
Ranch. William Cody architect. Presi-
dent Desert Laundry
Joan Cohn, 1001 N. Crescent Dr., Beverly
Hills. Paul R. Williams architect. Widow
of Harry Cohn, ex-wife of Laurence
Harvey
Stanley and Phyllis Goldberg, 2340 South-
ridge, William Cody architect. *Architectur-
al Digest*, Fall 1967. Chicago industrialist
Katherine (Betty) and Harry F. (Bud)
Haldeman, Smoke Tree Ranch, PS
William and Frances Hamling, 350 Via
Lola, PS. Elrod's 2nd house, sold fully
furnished and still intact
Harold and Mary Hicks, 860 Panorama
Rd., PS. Stewart Williams architect
Henry and Nancy Ittleson, 425 Via Lola,
PS. Howard Lapham architect. Former
home of Ernest and Leonore Alschuler
Maurice and Ruth Melamed, 37-361 Marx
Circle, Tamarisk CC, RM. William Cody
architect. Project #2.
Roy G. and Alta Woods, 7428 N. Coun-
try Club Dr., Nichols Hill, Oklahoma
City, OK. Howard Lapham architect.
House #1. *Architectural Digest*, Spring
1966. Founder, Woods Petroleum,
National Auto Transport Assoc., Star
Manufacturing

California DuPont room at the New York
World's Fair, 1964. With designer Doro-
thy Paul
8th Annual AAUW Tour. Homes of Joe
and Nelda Linsk, 470 W. Vista Chino,
Richard Neutra architect; Waldo and
Alice Avery, 335 W. Vereda Sur, William
Cody architect

International Design Center, 8899 Beverly
Blvd., West Hollywood. Morning room
exhibit

1965

Hazel Fairless, 98 Malibu Colony Road,
Malibu. *Architectural Digest*, Summer 1965
(cover only). Project #2
Myron E. and Rose Glass, 37–635 Palm
View Dr., Tamarisk CC, RM
Laurence Harvey, 419 Valmonte Sur, PS.
Elrod's first house. Project #2
Bob and Dolores Hope, 1188 El Alameda,
PS
Edwin "Buddy" and Carolyn Morris, 2203
Southridge, PS. Spec house built in
1964 by Thomas Griffing. Hugh Kaptur
architect. Sold to actor Steve McQueen
in 1969. Project #4
Michael and Gail Wolfson, 215 E. Chicago
Ave., Chicago. Project #1

Country Club Estates, 1987/89 S. Cami-
no Real, PS. A. Quincy Jones architect.
Model homes
Seven Lakes CC, 4100 Seven Lakes Dr.
Richard Harrison, architect. Model units
Tennis Club Homes, 555 W. Baristo Road.
William Cody architect. Model units
Ken Herman Real Estate, 1478 N. Palm
Canyon Dr. Office remodel
Eldorado Country Club Snack Bar
2nd Annual AID Interior Design Show
and Furniture Fashions Exposition, LA
Sports Arena. AID Pavilion exhibit by
U.S. Rubber Co. executed by Elrod

1966

Albert and Gertrude Baskin, 1002 Tama-
risk West, RM. House #2
Joseph and Doris Friend, 1012 Tamarisk
West, RM
Henry and Nancy Ittleson, Rien Ne Va Plus
villa, Roquebrune-Cap-Martin, French
Riviera
Irving and Ida Kay, 37–730 Da Vall Dr., RM
I.D. (Ike) and Rita Levy, 1550 Via Norte,
PS

Michael and Gail Wolfson, 1009 Tamarisk West, RM. Project #2

Rimcrest, 2110 Southridge Dr., PS. Renovation of complex and model units
Lee-Lasky development house, Escalon development, Encino. Dan Saxon Palmer, Palmer & Krisel, architect
10th Annual AAUW tour. Laurence Harvey, 419 Valmonte Sur. Elrod House #1

1967

Stephen Chase joins Arthur Elrod Associates
Otis and Lynn Booth, 1115 Oak Knoll Ave., San Marino. Executive, Times Mirror Co., Berkshire Hathaway investor
George and Marcia Barrett, 475 Vereda Norte, PS
Laurence Harvey, 475 Valmonte Sur, PS. House #3
Edwin J. and Georgia Heimer, 191 Merito Place, PS. House #3
Johnny and Lorene Revolta, 180 Desert Lakes Dr., Seven Lakes CC, PS. Professional golfer
Jeanette Edris Rockefeller, 657 Via Lola, PS. Daughter of William Edris and Frances Skinner; ex-wife of Arkansas governor Winthrop Rockefeller

International Design Center, 8899 Beverly Blvd., Los Angeles. *LA Times Home* magazine room, Jan 1, 1967
"Rooms of Tomorrow," 52nd National Hotel & Motel Exposition, New York Coliseum, Nov. 6–9. *New York Times,* Nov. 5, 1967
Committee of 25, O'Donnell Gate Lodge, PS. Stewart Williams remodel
Canyon Estates, 1453 Plato Circle, PS. Furnished model

11th Annual AAUW Annual home tour. Harold and Mary Hicks home, 860 Panorama Rd., PS

1968

Arthur Elrod Associates, 850 N. Palm Canyon Dr., PS. *LA Times Home,* June 16, 1968, *Interior Design,* Aug. 1968
Arthur Elrod, 2175 Southridge, PS. John Lautner architect. *LA Times Home,* Nov. 3, 1968; *House & Garden* May 1969; *Architectural Digest,* Spring 1969 (cover only); *Palm Springs Life,* Oct. 1969; *Architectural Digest,* Spring 1970; *Time,* March 29, 1971; *Playboy,* Nov. 1971
William and Barbara Foster, 603 La Mirada, PS. William Cody, architect. *Desert Sun,* Aug. 14, 1968, *Palm Springs Life,* Dec. 1968
David Greene, 2638 Kings Road East, PS
Pearl Helms, 1933 Galatea Terrace, Corona del Mar. House #2
Henry and Nancy Ittleson, 425 Via Lola (former Alschuler house). *LA Times Home* magazine, Oct. 19, 1969. Chairman and director CIT Financial Corp.
Mary and Jack Benny, 424 W. Vista Chino, PS. Tom and Anita May house. Edward Fickett architect
Edwin "Buddy" and Carolyn Morris, 875 Fifth Ave., NY. Project # 5
Nettie Wolf, 720 Camino Norte, PS

Mountain View Estates, corner of Via Monte Vista and Crescent Dr., PS. Alexander Construction Co. Model home
Plans for restaurant/nightclub, Palm Springs Municipal Airport
Galerie du Jonelle, 241 E. Tahquitz-McCallum Way, PS. Joe and Nelda Linsk. Project #2
1st Women's Architectural League Home Tour, chaired by Winifred Cody. Homes of Arthur Elrod, 2175 Southridge; Stanley and Phyllis Goldberg, 2340 Southridge; Joseph and Nelda Linsk, 470 W. Vista Chino

1969

Arthur Elrod, 289 Via Las Palmas, PS. Spec house. *House Beautiful,* April 1970. Sold to fashion designer James Galanos
M/M Michael Birnkrant, 619 Sarbonne Road, Bel-Air. Garrett Eckbo landscape architect
Barney and Harriet Hayden, 70–927 Fairway Dr., Tamarisk CC, RM. Buff & Hensman architects, John Krabbe landscape architect. *Architectural Digest,* Nov./ Dec. 1970
Georgia and Edwin Heimer, 470 Camino Norte, PS. Project #4
M/M John King, Eldorado CC, Indian Wells. William Cody architect. *Architectural Digest,* Jan./Feb. 1971
Henry B. and Babette Roth, 49505 Coachella Dr., La Quinta
Doris Warner Vidor, 591 W. Stevens Road, PS
Roy G. and Alta Woods, 40–995 Thunderbird Road, Thunderbird Heights, RM. Project #2. Former home of Hyatt Robert von Dehn, founder of Hyatt Hotels. *Architectural Digest,* Winter 1970, *National Design Center Guide: Home Decorating Ideas,* 1970.

Alan Ladd's Hardware, Sue Ladd, 500 S. Palm Canyon Dr., PS. Kaptur-Lapham architects
Mission Bay Properties, Mission Square, San Diego, William Hamling offices. *Interior Design,* Sept. 1969
13th Annual AAUW Home Tour, Elrod House, 2175 Southridge Dr.

1970

Frank and Lucille Capra, 49380 Avenida Fernando, La Quinta
Joseph and Wiki Dennis, 41915 Tonopah, Thunderbird Heights, RM. Ross Patten, Patten & Wild, architectural designer. *Palm Springs Life,* Sept. 1971

Sigmund E. Edelstone, Drake Towers, 179 Lake Shore Dr., Apt. 23E, Chicago. Ernest Grunsfeld III architect. *Architectural Digest*, May/June 1972. Project #1

Byron and Ruth Foster, 37–647 Palm View Rd, Tamarisk CC, RM. William Cody architect. LB Foster Co., Pittsburgh. House #1

Eunice and John Johnson, The Carlyle, 1040 N. Lake Shore Dr., Chicago. *Architectural Digest*, Nov./Dec. 1972. Founders Johnson Publishing Co. Project #1

M/M John King, 26 Sunset Dr., Englewood, CO. William Cody architect. House #2

Marion and E. Hadley Stuart, Jr., Diamond Dragon Ranch, Bellevue, ID. *L.A. Times* magazine Aug. 27, 1972. Carnation Milk Co. heir

Charles Naywert, Desert Fashion Plaza, PS. *Interior Design*, April 1971

Weifels & Sons, 666 Vella Road, PS

1971

Duane and Marsha Hagadone, Stanley Hill residence, corporate offices, and lake log house, Casco Bay, Coeur d'Alene, ID. *Architectural Digest*, Mar./Apr. 1974. *House Beautiful*, Sept. 1977

Martin Anthony Sinatra Medical Education Center, Desert Hospital, 500 E. Tachevah Dr., PS. Donald A. Wexler Associates architect. *Palm Springs Life*, March 1971

Desert Hospital remodeled lobby, PS

1972

Louis T. and Marion Brody, 1040 Lake Shore Dr., Chicago

M/M Robert Brown, 2477 Southridge Dr., PS. Buff & Hensman architects, former William Holden house

Byron and Ruth Foster, Gateway Towers, 320 Fort Duquesne Blvd., Pittsburgh, PA. House #2

David Janssen, Century Towers West, 2220 Avenue of the Stars, Century City. Actor

Nelda and Joe Linsk, 425 Camino Norte, PS. Tennis Pavilion by William Cody. Project #3

Edwin "Buddy" Morris, Dorset Hotel, New York. Project #6

Roland and Ramona Sahm, Del Dios Ranch, Rancho Santa Fe, CA. Fred Briggs architect. *Architectural Digest*, July/Aug. 1976, *Moving House & Home*, Winter 1981

Louise and Lionel Steinberg, 300 Merito Place, PS. Buff & Hensman architects. Built for actor Laurence Harvey. *Interior Design*, June 1976

Johnson Publishing Company, 820 S. Michigan Ave., Chicago. John Moutoussamy architect. *Ebony*, Sept. 1972, *Interior Design*, Oct. 1972. Project #2

John Strauss showroom, Chicago

That John's Restaurant, El Paseo, PD

1973

M/M Daniel Bernheim, 69 Crest Dr., South Orange, NJ

M/M Alex Coleman, Beverly Hills

Sigmund E. Edelstone, 130 W. Racquet Club Road, PS. Project #2. *Architectural Digest*, Sept./Oct. 1975

Alfred and Monte Goldman, 525 Portlock Road, Oahu, Hawaii. Former Henry + Alyce Kaiser estate. *Architectural Digest*, July/Aug. 1974 and Jan./Feb. 1976. Oklahoma real estate developers

Milton and Dorothy Feldmar, 1206 Tamarisk West, RM

Henry and Nancy Ittleson, Hotel Pierre #807, NY. Project #3

Irving and Ida Kay, 166 Geary St., San Francisco

Charles and Liz Koch, 1400 N. Woodlawn, Wichita, KS, and The Lodge, Vail townhouse. Chairman Koch Industries

F. Pierce and Fay Lathrop, 40–460 Via Entrada, Thunderbird Heights, RM. Founder Lathrop Construction

James and Ruth Meade, 71–136 La Paz, Tamarisk CC, RM. Buff & Hensman architects

Edwin "Buddy" and Carolyn Morris, 775 Mission Road, PS. Project #7

Jean Nidetch, 12002 Benmore Terrace, Brentwood. Eugene Stephenson architect. Cofounder Weight Watchers

Palm Springs Desert Museum, 101 Museum Dr., PS. Stewart Williams architect

Lockheed Jet-Star jet, Esmark Inc., Chicago, and AiResearch, Los Angeles

David Greene, Diplomat Condominium Models, 1630 La Reina, E. Palm Canyon Dr., PS

Twin Springs Condominiums, 2696 Sierra Madre, PS. Land planning, site design, architecture and engineering by Donald A. Wexler Associates. Three model units plus clubhouse furnished by Elrod

Desert Dorado, 503 Lujo, PS. Hugh Kaptur, Kaptur-Latham Associates, architect. Model home

Cricket Club, 1800 NE 114th St., Miami. Model condo unit

1974

All projects that were near completion or in the works after Arthur Elrod's death in February 1974 were finished by Hal Broderick and Steve Chase

p. 2 George R. Szanik/George Szanik papers (Collection 1799), Library Special Collections, Charles E. Young Research Library, UCLA

p. 4 Fritz Taggart

p. 7 George R. Szanik/George Szanik papers (Collection 1799), Library Special Collections, Charles E. Young Research Library, UCLA

p. 11 Courtesy Michael Calloway

p. 12 Julius Shulman © J. Paul Getty Trust. Getty Research Institute, Los Angeles (2004.R.10)

p. 13 Courtesy Michael Calloway

p. 14 *Desert Sun*

p. 15 Julius Shulman © J. Paul Getty Trust. Getty Research Institute, Los Angeles (2004.R.10)

p. 16 Harold C. Broderick/Arthur Elrod Associates, Inc. Collection, Palm Springs Art Museum, 15-2007

p. 17 Hartsook, San Francisco. Courtesy Michael Calloway (headshot). Harold C. Broderick/Arthur Elrod Associates, Inc. Collection, Palm Springs Art Museum, 15-2007 (diagram)

p. 18 + 19 Moulin Studios. Harold C. Broderick/Arthur Elrod Associates, Inc. Collection, Palm Springs Art Museum, 15-2007

p. 21 Harold C. Broderick/Arthur Elrod Associates, Inc. Collection, Palm Springs Art Museum, 15-2007

p. 23 Ernest Silva. Harold C. Broderick/Arthur Elrod Associates, Inc. Collection, Palm Springs Art Museum, 15-2007

p. 25, 26, 27 Julius Shulman © J. Paul Getty Trust. Getty Research Institute, Los Angeles (2004.R.10)

p. 29 Courtesy Michael Calloway

p. 30 George R. Szanik/George Szanik papers (Collection 1799), Library Special Collections, Charles E. Young Research Library, UCLA

p. 32, 33, 34, 35 John Hartley. Harold C. Broderick/Arthur Elrod Associates, Inc. Collection, Palm Springs Art Museum, 15-2007

p. 36, 37, 38 Maynard L. Parker, photographer. Courtesy of The Huntington Library, San Marino, California.

p. 39 Carl Junghans

p. 40, 41, 42, 43 George R. Szanik/George Szanik papers (Collection 1799), Library Special Collections, Charles E. Young Research Library, UCLA

p. 44 Victor Culina ("before"), Harold C. Broderick/Arthur Elrod Associates, Inc. Collection, Palm Springs Art Museum, 15-2007. George R. Szanik/George Szanik papers (Collection 1799), Library Special Collections, Charles E. Young Research Library, UCLA (photo). Artist unknown, Harold C. Broderick/Arthur Elrod Associates, Inc. Collection, Palm Springs Art Museum, 15-2007 (ink wash)

p. 45, 46, 47 George R. Szanik/George Szanik papers (Collection 1799), Library Special Collections, Charles E. Young Research Library, UCLA

p. 48, 49 Julius Shulman © J. Paul Getty Trust. Getty Research Institute, Los Angeles (2004.R.10)

p. 50, 51 George R. Szanik/George Szanik papers (Collection 1799), Library Special Collections, Charles E. Young Research Library, UCLA

p. 52 Courtesy Catherine Cody Nemirovsky

p. 54, 55 Julius Shulman © J. Paul Getty Trust. Getty Research Institute, Los Angeles (2004.R.10)

p. 57 George R. Szanik, Copyright 1958. *Los Angeles Times*. Used with Permission (top). Victor Culina, Palm Springs Life (bottom)

p. 58, 59 Harold C. Broderick/Arthur Elrod Associates, Inc. Collection, Palm Springs Art Museum, 15-2007

p. 62, 63, 64, 65 George de Gennaro, Copyright 1958. *Los Angeles Times*. Used with Permission

p. 67 Richard R. Hewett. Copyright 1959. *Los Angeles Times*. Used with Permission

p. 69, 70 Julius Shulman, © J. Paul Getty Trust. Getty Research Institute, Los Angeles (2004.R.10)

p. 71 George R. Szanik/George Szanik papers (Collection 1799), Library Special Collections, Charles E. Young Research Library, UCLA

p. 72, 73 George R. Szanik/George Szanik papers (Collection 1799), Library Special Collections, Charles E. Young Research Library, UCLA

p. 74 Julius Shulman, © J. Paul Getty Trust. Getty Research Institute, Los Angeles (2004.R.10) (left). George R. Szanik/George Szanik papers (Collection 1799), Library Special Collections, Charles E. Young Research Library, UCLA (right)

p. 75 George R. Szanik/George Szanik papers (Collection 1799), Library Special Collections, Charles E. Young Research Library, UCLA

p. 76 Julius Shulman, © J. Paul Getty Trust. Getty Research Institute, Los Angeles (2004.R.10)

p. 77 Shaw-Poinc

p. 78 Photo by Slim Aarons/Hulton Archive/Getty Images

p. 81 Harold C. Broderick/Arthur Elrod Associates, Inc. Collection, Palm Springs Art Museum, 15-2007

p. 82, 83 Julius Shulman, © J. Paul Getty Trust. Getty Research Institute, Los Angeles (2004.R.10)

p. 84 Robert Phillips/Courtesy Nelda Linsk

p. 85, 86, 87 Courtesy Nelda Linsk

p. 88 Val Samuelson. Harold C. Broderick/Arthur Elrod Associates, Inc. Collection, Palm Springs Art Museum, 15-2007 ("before"). George R. Szanik/George Szanik papers (Collection 1799), Library Special Collections, Charles E. Young Research Library, UCLA

p. 89, 90 George R. Szanik/George Szanik papers (Collection 1799), Library Special Collections, Charles E. Young Research Library, UCLA

p. 91 Adele Cygelman

p. 92 David Glomb

p. 93 George R. Szanik/George Szanik papers (Collection 1799), Library Special Collections, Charles E. Young Research Library, UCLA

p. 94 George Aquino/Palm Springs Historical Society

p. 95 Paul Pospesil Collection/Palm Springs Historical Society (portrait), Leland Y. Lee (interiors)

p. 96 Julius Shulman, © J. Paul Getty Trust. Getty Research Institute, Los Angeles (2004.R.10), George de Gennaro

p. 97 Fritz Taggart (above), David Glomb (below), George R. Szanik/George Szanik papers (Collection 1799), Library Special Collections, Charles E. Young Research Library, UCLA (right)

p. 98, 99 Harold C. Broderick/Arthur Elrod Associates, Inc. Collection, Palm Springs Art Museum, 15-2007

p. 100, 101, 102 David Glomb

p. 103 David Glomb (left), Courtesy Michael Calloway (right)

p. 104 Horst Ahlberg. Harold C. Broderick/Arthur Elrod Associates, Inc. Collection, Palm Springs Art Museum, 15-2007. George R. Szanik/George Szanik papers (Collection 1799), Library Special Collections, Charles E. Young Research Library, UCLA

p. 105, 106, 107, 108, 110, 111, 112 George R. Szanik/George Szanik papers (Collection 1799), Library Special Collections, Charles E. Young Research Library, UCLA

p. 114 Fritz Taggart. Harold C. Broderick/Arthur Elrod Associates, Inc. Collection, Palm Springs Art Museum, 15-2007

p. 115, 116, 117, 118, 119 George R. Szanik/George Szanik papers (Collection 1799), Library Special Collections, Charles E. Young Research Library, UCLA. J.R. Eyerman. Harold C. Broderick/Arthur Elrod Associates, Inc. Collection, Palm Springs Art Museum, 15-2007 (portraits).

p. 120 Harold C. Broderick/Arthur Elrod Associates, Inc. Collection, Palm Springs Art Museum, 15-2007 (portrait), George R. Szanik/George Szanik papers (Collection 1799), Library Special Collections, Charles E. Young Research Library, UCLA

p. 121, 122, 123, 124, 125, 126, 127, 128 George R. Szanik/George Szanik papers (Collection 1799), Library Special Collections, Charles E. Young Research Library, UCLA

p. 129, 130, 131, 132, 133 Leland Y. Lee. Harold C. Broderick/Arthur Elrod Associates, Inc. Collection, Palm Springs Art Museum, 15-2007

p. 134 Fritz Taggart

p. 137 Harold C. Broderick/Arthur Elrod Associates, Inc. Collection, Palm Springs Art Museum, 15-2007

p. 138 E. Stewart Williams. Harold C. Broderick/Arthur Elrod Associates, Inc. Collection, Palm Springs Art Museum, 15-2007

p. 139 Harold C. Broderick/Arthur Elrod Associates, Inc. Collection, Palm Springs Art Museum, 15-2007

p. 140, 141, 142, 143 Leland Y. Lee. Harold C. Broderick/Arthur Elrod Associates, Inc. Collection, Palm Springs Art Museum, 15-2007

p. 144, 145, 146, 147, 148, 149 Fritz Taggart

p. 150, 151, 152, 153, 154, 155, 156, 157 Alexandre Georges. Harold C. Broderick/Arthur Elrod Associates, Inc. Collection, Palm Springs Art Museum, 15-2007

p. 158, 159 Leland Y. Lee Harold C. Broderick/Arthur Elrod Associates, Inc. Collection, Palm Springs Art Museum, 15-2007

p. 160, 161, 162, 163, 164, 165, 166, 167, 168, 169, 170, 171, 172, 173 Fritz Taggart

p. 174, 175, 176, 178, 179 Ernest Silva. Harold C. Broderick/Arthur Elrod Associates, Inc. Collection, Palm Springs Art Museum, 15-2007

p. 181, 182 Leland Y. Lee

p. 183, 184, 185 John Lautner Archive, Research Library, Getty Research Institute, LA © 2018 The John Lautner Foundation

p. 186, 188, 189, 190, 191, 192, 193, 194, 195 Leland Y. Lee

p. 196 Richard Gross

p. 197 Leland Y. Lee (left), Mario Casilli (right). Archival Playboy Magazine material. Copyright 1971 by Playboy. Used with permission. All rights reserved.

p. 198, 199 Leland Y. Lee

p. 200 Richard Gross. Copyright 1968. *Los Angeles Times*. Used with Permission

p. 201, 202 Leland Y. Lee

p. 203 Julian Wasser (left)

p. 204 John Lautner Archive, Research Library, Getty Research Institute, LA © 2018 The John Lautner Foundation

p. 205 Tycho Saariste

p. 206 Guy Webster

p. 207 John Lautner Archive, Research Library, Getty Research Institute, LA © 2018 The John Lautner Foundation

p. 209 Photos by Anwar Hussein/Hulton Archive/Getty Images

"A View to Thrill" by Timothy Braseth, *Modernism* magazine, Summer 2012

Accessing the Past, www.accessingthepast.org.

Architectural Design, May 1969.

Architectural Digest, Fall 1962 (Vol. XIX, No. 3), Winter 1963 (Vol. XIX, No. 4), Spring 1963, Summer 1965 (cover only), Spring 1966 (Vol. XXII, No. 4), Fall 1967, Spring 1969 (cover only), Winter 1970, Spring 1970, November/December 1970, May/June 1972, November/December 1972, May/June 1973, March/April 1974, September/October 1975.

Architectural Record, May 1963, November 1970.

Birmingham, Stephen. *Certain People: America's Black Elite.* Little Brown & Co., 1977.

Bricker, Lauren Weiss, and Sidney Williams. *Steel and Shade: The Architecture of Donald Wexler.* Kehrer Heidelberg, 2011.

Cohen, Bette Jane. *The Spirit in Architecture: John Lautner*, documentary film, 1991.

Cygelman, Adele, and David Glomb. *Palm Springs Modern.* Rizzoli, 1999.

"Decorators: The Mix Masters." *Time*, February 9, 1968.

Desert Sun, 1948–74. Accessible online at California Digital Newspaper Collection, www.cdnc.ucr.edu.

Design in the Desert: Arthur Elrod, Architecture and Design Council Lecture Series, February 12, 2005.

Ebony, September 1972.

Escher, Frank. *John Lautner, Architect.* Princeton Architectural Press, 1998.

Hensman, Donald C., FAIA, and James Steele, ed. *Buff & Hensman.* Balcony Press, 2005.

Hess, Alan, and Alan Weintraub. *The Architecture of John Lautner.* Rizzoli, 2000.

House & Garden, May 1969.

House Beautiful, March 1958, September 1977.

"How the Other Half Bathes." *Time*, March 29, 1971.

Interior Design, June 1954, August 1963, August 1968, June 1969, April 1971, November/December 1972, June 1976.

Iovine, Julie, and Todd Merrill. Chapter on Arthur Elrod by Peter Wolf. *Modern Americana: Studio Furniture from High Craft to High Glam.* Rizzoli, 2008.

Johnson, John H. *Succeeding Against the Odds: the Inspiring Autobiography of One of America's Wealthiest Entrepreneurs.* Warner Books, 1989.

Los Angeles Times Home Magazine, 1955–74. http://latimes.newspapers.com.

Menrad, Chris, and Heidi Creighton, eds. *William Krisel's Palm Springs: The Language of Modernism.* Gibbs Smith, 2016.

"New Designs for Living." *Newsweek*, January 22, 1973.

Palm Springs Life, 1959–74.

"Palm Springs Portrait." *Town & Country*, February 1978.

Palm Springs Villager, 1948–59.

Playboy, November 1971.

Smart, George. *North Carolina Modernist Houses*, www.ncmodernist.org.

Sinatra, Barbara. *Lady Blue Eyes: My Life with Frank.* Three Rivers Press, 2012.

Sausalito News, April 16, 1954.

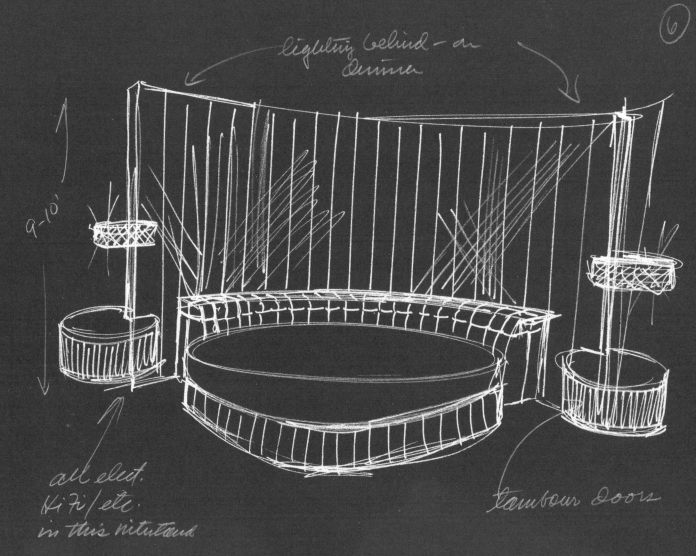

lighting behind — on
dimmer

6

9-10'

all elect.
HiFi/etc.
in this nitestand

tambour doors

for lacquer finish

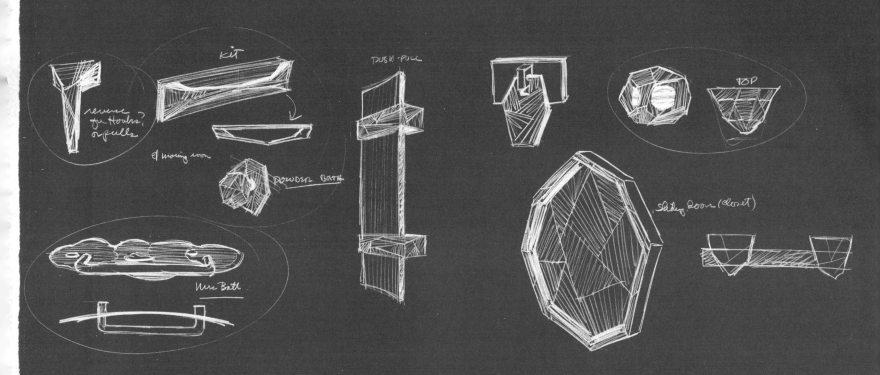

KIT

reverse for hooks?
or pulls

El moving room

POWDER BATH

DUSK-PULL

TOP

Mrs Bath

Sliding doors (closet)

ORGAN

BEHIND DOORS
STORAGE

COPL of
METAL?

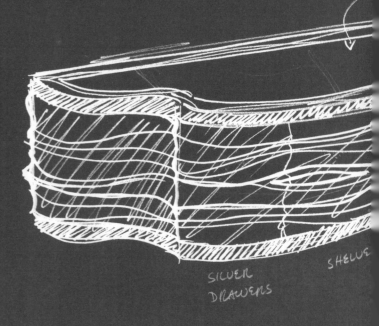

SILVER
DRAWERS

SHELVE